a

SECOND
SELECTIONS FROM
MODERN POETS

SECOND
SELECTIONS FROM
MODERN POETS

MADE BY SIR JOHN SQUIRE

NINTH IMPRESSION

LONDON :
MARTIN SECKER
& WARBURG LTD.
1941

First published November 1924
Reprinted   November 1924
Reprinted   December 1925
Reprinted   October 1926
Reprinted   April 1927
Reprinted   January 1929
Reprinted   February 1932
Reprinted   May 1937
Reprinted   January 1941

THE DUNEDIN PRESS, LIMITED, EDINBURGH

PREFACE

The volume, *Selections from Modern Poets*, of which this is a sequel, was an attempt to illustrate the work which had been done by the younger English poets. It included poems by men living and dead. A man's contemporaneousness is not governed by the accident of survival; the dead who died young were more " modern " than their elders who survived them for years; so I took a date of birth and made that my line of division. I included nothing by any poet, living or dead, who had been born before 1870. That was resolved in 1919; I have now moved my date on by five years; and the present collection includes no work by anyone who will be, or if living would have been, fifty before 1924 has ended.

This means that some of the best known names in the first volume will not be found here. The loss of many fine poems may be compensated for by the presence of much interesting work by the youngest generation of writers. About half of my first list do not reappear; some because they have passed the age-limit, some because they have written nothing recently, some because they were already dead five years ago. In their place will be found as many more, including one or two dead soldiers whose work I did not know when I made my last selections.

For a general statement of my object in bringing these

PREFACE

poems together I must refer the reader to my former preface. What I said then I still believe; and if, so far as the general body of readers is concerned, there seems to-day less eagerness than there was to welcome the work of young poets, I feel all the more strongly the obligation to call attention to its merits. I cannot hope that any other person will think I have included all the good poems that I might have found, or that there are no weaknesses in the selection I have actually made.

For leave to print copyright poems I am indebted to Messrs Blackwood (Alfred Noyes); Bowes & Bowes (J. R. Ackerley, A. Y. Campbell, Edward Davison, Frank Kendon, J. B. Priestley); R. Cobden-Sanderson (Edmund Blunden and J. Middleton Murry); Constable & Co. (Rose Macaulay and P. H. B. Lyon); Collins Sons & Co. (Edward Shanks and Gerald Gould); Chatto & Windus (Wilfred Owen and Robert Nichols); Christophers (F. V. Branford); Heinemann (Robert Graves, John Masefield, Dorothy Wellesley); Hodder & Stoughton (Paul Bewsher); John Lane (Kenneth Ashley and Frank Kendon); Macmillan & Co. (W. W. Gibson); Elkin Mathews (G. R. Hamilton); John Murray (Geoffrey Dearmer); Oxford University Press (J. D. C. Pellow); Cecil Palmer (E. N. da C. Andrade); Poetry Bookshop (Harold Monro and Frances Cornford); Sidgwick & Jackson (Edmund Blunden, John Drinkwater and Jeffery Day); Secker (Robert Graves, Martin Armstrong and D. H. Lawrence).

J. C. Squire.

J. R. ACKERLEY

A

THE PORTRAIT OF A MOTHER

Your calm eyes watch me as I pace the floor;
Across the room and back they follow me :
Calm eyes, calm eyes, what do you watch me for;
    Calm eyes that cannot see?

There is some hidden meaning in your gaze,
Which sweeps and swells upon me like a tide :
There is some word, some swift elusive phrase
    Between your lips has died.

There is a kind of horror in your stare,
As though you shrank in fear from something
    strange.
'Tis but my fancy. It was never there,
    And portraits do not change.

O watch me not ! In quest of solitude
I turn among the shadows as I pace;
But I have not the power to elude
    The vigil of your face.

I move away, you follow with your gaze;
I steal a glance, your eyes are watching me;
I scan your face, no movement it betrays . . .
    They turn so stealthily.

'Tis but a trick that any can disprove,
A simple fraud, a trick of pose and light.
Calm eyes, behind that glass you cannot move;
    Calm eyes, you have no sight.

Your power is gone. In me you have no part.
The babe you suckled and remembered still
Whene'er you took the schoolboy to your heart
    Is stranger to your will.

What do you see? That fixed, relentless look
Searching my visage seems to learn from it.
The face of man is not an open book
    In which his sins are writ.

My face betrays no secrets; Saturn ploughs
The lines upon the skin in other wise;
The vilest thoughts are hived in tranquil brows
    And peep from tranquil eyes.

4

You look and shrink . . . as though I had
    betrayed
Some sacred trust laid on me by a child;
Or smothered Love in secret as he played,
       Smothered him as he smiled.

Why do you move beside me as I move?
O close your eyes and shut my thoughts from me!
It was too beautiful . . . the face of Love . . .
       For my mortality.

E. N. DA C. ANDRADE

WITH A COPY OF THE FAITHFUL
SHEPHERDESS

Too plain for this accomplisht age
Our Fletcher's fresh and simple page :
Too crude and gross-improbable
The faery deeds he turns to tell :
Too frail by far such fancies, vain
Such themes, not to be heard again.

—But be you so at war with time
As still to love once-honoured rhyme,
O, be you such as song can please
You shall hear such harmonies,
Such melody of concènt meet
As Nature makes with influence sweet
Or a summer afternoon ;
Or as the resplendent moon
Draws from all the silver-blue
Countryside, when clouds are few.

Come, take hands, you are not such
As this will weary overmuch.
Sit we down, and hear rehearse
The marvels of the sweet-souled verse,
All the works that wonderly
Befel the night in Thessaly.
Keep holy silence, meed no less
Is due the FAITHFUL SHEPHERDESS.

E. N. DA C. ANDRADE

FATE AND THE LITTLE FLOWERS

You know the wild flowers suit your hair :
Place hands full of the purple bloom
Of loosestrife, glad of such soft doom,
And tender-toned narcissus there ;

Green leaves and wind-flowers, take them all.
As fate that rules us, sweet, be blind
In this your choice, nor, as you bind,
Care which hold fast, while others fall—

Fall to be trodden underfoot,
Though all ways fair as those you take,
Or those that in the neighbouring brake
Still suck sweet moisture from the root.

A SONG FOR EDMUND BLUNDEN

THE BOY AND THE BIRDS

" You little birds, so free from care,
Who slide on the supporting air
As I do on this slope of green,
And peck the dirt, but keep you clean,

Who drink bright dew, and when you will
On grain and grass seed eat your fill,
And see when berries first are red,
Looking on trees from overhead,

What are the secrets that you sing
So blithely; from what journeying
Do you take rest when day is done? "
A brown bird answered him anon—

" We are not clean, the dirt we peck
Cleaves to the feathers of the neck;
Men walk on earth, and in the air
Hawks fly, we are not free from care.

12

Your father bears an iron reed
Filled with a flame that makes us bleed;
Your kindly mother loves to tear
Feathers and skin to deck her hair.

Memories of winter want make keen
The songs we sing now leaves are green.
Victims of many a strange deceiving
We sing lest death should catch us grieving."

—He ceased, and with an artful note
Of sweets and shrills composed his throat.
And I have set down what I heard
From this philosophising bird.

MARTIN ARMSTRONG

IN LAMPLIGHT

Now that the chill October day is declining,
Pull the blinds, draw each voluminous curtain
Till the room is full of gloom and of the uncertain
Gleams of firelight on polished edges shining.
Then bring the rosy lamp to its wonted station
On the dark-gleaming table. In that soft
    splendour
Well-known things of the room, grown deep and
    tender,
Gather around, a mysterious congregation :—
Pallid sheen of silver, the bright brass fender,
The wine-red pool of carpet, the bowl of roses
Lustrous-hearted, crimsons and purples looming
From dusky rugs and curtains. Nothing dis-
    closes
The unseen walls but the broken, richly-glooming
Gold of frames and opulent wells of mingling
Dim colours gathered in darkened mirrors. And
    breaking

17

The dreamlike spell and out of your deep chair
    moving
You go, perhaps to the shelves and, slowly
    singling
Some old rich-blazoned book, return. But the
    gleaming
Spells close round you again and you fall to
    dreaming,
Eyes grown dim, the book on your lap unheeded.

MISS THOMPSON GOES SHOPPING

Miss Thompson at Home

In her lone cottage on the downs,
With winds and blizzards and great crowns
Of shining cloud, with wheeling plover
And short grass sweet with the small white
    clover,
Miss Thompson lived, correct and meek,
A lonely spinster, and every week
On market-day she used to go
Into the little town below,
Tucked in the great downs' hollow bowl,
Like pebbles gathered in a shoal.

She Goes a-Marketing

So, having washed her plates and cup
And banked the kitchen fire up,
Miss Thompson slipped upstairs and dressed,
Put on her black (her second best),

19

The bonnet trimmed with rusty plush,
Peeped in the glass with simpering blush,
From camphor-smelling cupboard took
Her thicker jacket off the hook
Because the day might turn to cold.
Then, ready, slipped downstairs and rolled
The hearthrug back; then searched about,
Found her basket, ventured out,
Snecked the door and paused to lock it
And plunged the key in some deep pocket.
Then as she tripped demurely down
The steep descent, the little town
Spread wider till its sprawling street
Enclosed her and her footfalls beat
On hard stone pavement; and she felt
Those throbbing ecstasies that melt
Through heart and mind as, happy, free,
Her small, prim personality
Merged into the seething strife
Of auction-marts and city life.

She Visits the Bootmaker

Serenely down the busy stream
Miss Thompson floated in a dream.
Now, hovering beelike, she would stop
Entranced before some tempting shop,

Getting in people's way and prying
At things she never thought of buying;
Now wafted on without an aim.
And thus in course of time she came
To Watson's bootshop. Long she pries
At boots and shoes of every size,
Brown football boots, with bar and stud,
For boys that scuffle in the mud,
And dancing-pumps with pointed toes
Glassy as jet, and dull black bows;
Slim ladies' shoes with two-inch heel,
And sprinkled beads of gold and steel.
" How anyone can wear such things ! "
On either side the doorway springs
(As in a tropic jungle loom
Masses of strange thick-petalled bloom
And fruits misshapen) fold on fold
A growth of sandshoes rubber-soled,
Clambering the doorposts, branching, spawn-
    ing
Their barbarous bunches like an awning
Over the windows and the doors.

Is Tempted

But, framed among the other stores,
Something has caught Miss Thompson's eye

(O worldliness, O vanity !),
A pair of slippers—scarlet plush.
Miss Thompson feels a conscious blush
Suffuse her face, as though her thought
Had ventured further than it ought.
But O that colour's rapturous singing
And the answer in her lone heart ringing !
She turns (O, Guardian Angels, stop her
From doing anything improper !).
She turns; and, see, she stoops and bungles
In through the sandshoes' hanging jungles,
Away from light and common-sense,
Into the shop dim-lit and dense
With smells of polish and tanned hide.
Soon from a dark recess inside
Fat Mrs Watson comes, slip slop,
To mind the business of the shop.
She walks flat-footed with a roll—
A serviceable, homely soul,
With kindly, ugly face like dough,
Hair dull and colourless as tow.
A huge Scotch pebble fills the space
Between her bosom and her face.
One sees her making beds all day.
Miss Thompson lets her say her say

—" So chilly for the time of year.
It's ages since we saw you here "—
Then, heart a-flutter, speech precise,
Describes the shoes and asks the price.
" Them, miss? Ah, them is six-and-nine ! "

Wrestles with the Temptation

Miss Thompson shudders down the spine
(Dream of impossible romance).
She eyes them with a wistful glance,
Torn between good and evil. Yes,
For half-a-minute, and no less,
Miss Thompson strives with seven devils,
Then, soaring over earthly levels,
Turns from the shoes with lingering touch—

And is Saved

" Ah, six-and-nine is far too much !
Sorry to trouble you. Good-day ! "

She Visits the Fishmonger

A little further down the way
Stands Miles's fish shop, whence is shed
So strong a smell of fishes dead

That people of a subtler sense
Hold their breath and hurry thence.
Miss Thompson hovers there and gazes.
Her housewife's knowing eye appraises
Salt and fresh, severely cons
Kippers bright as tarnished bronze;
Great cods disposed upon the sill,
Chilly and wet with gaping gill,
Flat head, glazed eye, and mute, uncouth,
Shapeless, wan, old-woman's mouth.
Next, a row of soles and plaice,
With querulous and twisted face,
And red-eyed bloaters, golden-grey;
Smoked haddocks ranked in neat array;
A group of smelts that take the light
Like slips of rainbow, pearly bright;
Silver trout with rosy spots,
And coral shrimps with keen black dots
For eyes, and hard and jointed sheath
And crisp tails curving underneath.
But there upon the sanded floor,
More wonderful in all that store
Than anything on slab or shelf,
Stood Miles the fishmonger himself.
Foursquare he stood and filled the place.
His huge hands and his jolly face

Were red. He had a mouth to quaff
Pint after pint : a sounding laugh,
But wheezy at the end, and oft
His eyes bulged outwards and he coughed.
Aproned he stood from chin to toe.
The apron's vertical long flow
Warped grandly outwards to display
His hale, round belly hung midway,
Whose apex was securely bound
With apron-strings wrapped round and round.
Outside Miss Thompson, small and staid,
Felt, as she always felt, afraid
Of this huge man who laughed so loud
And drew the notice of the crowd.
Awhile she paused in timid thought,
Then promptly hurried in and bought
" Two kippers, please. Yes, lovely weather."
" Two kippers? Sixpence altogether."
And in her basket laid the pair
Wrapped face to face in newspaper.

Relapses into Temptation

Then on she went, as one half blind,
For things were stirring in her mind.
Then turned about with fixed intent,
And, heading for the bootshop, went

And Falls

Straight in and bought the scarlet slippers,
And popped them in beside the kippers.

She Visits the Chemist

So much for that. From there she tacked,
Still flushed by this decisive act,
Westward, and came without a stop
To Mr Wren the chemist's shop,
And paused outside a while to see
The tall, big-bellied bottles, three—
Red, blue, and emerald, richly bright,
Each with its burning core of light.
The bell chimed as she pushed the door,
Spotless the oilcloth on the floor,
Limpid as water each glass case,
Each thing precisely in its place.
Rows of small drawers, black-lettered each
With curious words of foreign speech,
Ranked high above the other ware.
The old strange fragrance filled the air,
A fragrance like the garden pink,
But tinged with vague medicinal stink

Of camphor, soap, new sponges, blent
With chloroform and violet scent.
And Wren the chemist tall and spare
Stood gaunt behind his counter there.
Quiet and very wise he seemed,
With skull-like face, bald head that gleamed;
Through spectacles his eyes looked kind;
He wore a pencil tucked behind
His ear. And never he mistakes
The wildest signs the doctor makes
Prescribing drugs. Brown paper, string
He will not use for anything,
But all in neat white parcels packs
And sticks them up with sealing wax.
Miss Thompson bowed and blushed, and then
Undoubting bought of Mr Wren,
Being free from modern scepticism,
A bottle for her rheumatism,
Also some peppermints to take
In case of wind; an oval cake
Of scented soap; a penny square
Of pungent naphthalene to scare
The moth. And after Wren had wrapped
And sealed the lot, Miss Thompson clapped
Them in beside the fish and shoes.
" Good-day," she says, and off she goes.

Is Led Away by the Pleasure of the Town

Bee-like Miss Thompson, whither next?
Outside you pause awhile, perplext,
Your bearings lost. Then all comes back
And round she wheels, hot on the track
Of Giles the grocer; and from there
To Emilie the milliner,
There to be tempted by the sight
Of hats and blouses fiercely bright.
(O guard Miss Thompson, Powers that Be,
From Crudeness and Vulgarity!)
Still on from shop to shop she goes
With sharp bird's-eye, inquiring nose,
Prying and peering, entering some,
Oblivious of the thought of home.

Is Convinced of Indiscretion

The town brimmed up with deep-blue haze,
But still she stayed to flit and gaze,
Her eyes a-blur with rapturous sights,
Her small soul full of small delights,
Empty her purse, her basket filled.
The traffic in the town was stilled.
The clock struck six. Men thronged the inns.
Dear, dear, she should be home long since.

28

And Returns Home

Then as she climbed the misty downs
The lamps were lighted in the town's
Small streets. She saw them star by star
Multiplying from afar;
Till, mapped beneath her, she could trace
Each street and the wide, square market place
Sunk deep and deeper as she went
Higher up the steep ascent.
And all that soul-uplifting stir
Step by step fell back from her,
The glory gone, the blossoming
Shrivelled, and she, a small, frail thing,
Carrying her laden basket. Till
Darkness and silence of the hill
Received her in their restful care
And stars came dropping through the air.

But loudly, sweetly sang the slippers
In the basket with the kippers,
And loud and sweet the answering thrills
From her lone heart on the hills.

HONEY HARVEST

Late in March, when the days are growing longer
And sight of early green
Tells of the coming spring and suns grown
    stronger,
Round the pale willow-catkins there are seen
  The year's first honey-bees
Stealing the nectar : and bee-masters know
This for the first sign of the honey-flow.

Then in the dark hillsides the Cherry-trees
Gleam white with loads of blossom where the
    gleams
Of piled snow lately hung, and richer streams
The honey. Now, if chilly April days
Delay the Apple blossom and the May's
First week come in with sudden summer weather,
The Apple and the Hawthorn bloom together,
And all day long the plundering hordes go round
And every overweighted blossom nods.
But from that gathered essence they compound
Honey more sweet than nectar of the gods.

Those blossoms fall ere June, warm June that
    brings
The small white Clover. Field by scented field,
Round farms like islands in the rolling weald,
It spreads thick-flowering or in wildness springs
Short-stemmed upon the naked downs, to yield
A richer store of honey than the Rose,
The Pink, the Honeysuckle. Thence there flows
Nectar of clearest amber, redolent
    Of every flowery scent
That the warm wind upgathers as he goes.

In mid-July be ready for the noise
Of million bees in old Lime-avenues,
As though hot noon had found a droning voice
To ease her soul. Here for those busy crews
Green leaves and pale-stemmed clusters of green
    flowers
Build heavy-perfumed, cool, green-twilight bowers
Whence, load by load, through the long summer
    days
    They fill their glassy cells
With dark green honey, clear as chrysoprase,
Which housewives shun; but the bee-master tells
This brand is more delicious than all else.

In August-time, if moors are near at hand,
Be wise and in the evening-twilight load
Your hives upon a cart, and take the road
By night : that, ere the early dawn shall spring
And all the hills turn rosy with the Ling,
   Each waking hive may stand
Established in its new appointed land
Without harm taken, and the earliest flights
Set out at once to loot the heathery heights.

That vintage of the heather yields so dense
And glutinous a syrup that it foils
Him who would spare the comb and drain from
    thence
   Its dark, full-flavoured spoils :
For he must squeeze to wreck the beautiful
Frail edifice. Not otherwise he sacks
Those many chambered palaces of wax.

Then let a choice of every kind be made
And, labelled, set upon your storehouse racks—
Of Hawthorn-honey that of almond smacks :
The luscious Lime-tree-honey green as jade :
Pale Willow-honey, hived by the first rover :
   That delicate honey culled

From Apple-blossom, that of sunlight tastes :
And sunlight-coloured honey of the Clover.
  Then, when the late year wastes,
When night falls early and the moon is dulled
  And the last warm days are over,
Unlock the store, and to your table bring
Essence of every blossom of the spring.
And if, when wind has never ceased to blow
All night, you wake to roofs and trees becalmed
  In level wastes of snow,
Bring out the Lime-tree-honey, the embalmed
Soul of a lost July, or Heather-spiced
Brown-gleaming comb wherein sleeps crystallised
All the hot perfume of the heathery slope.
And, tasting and remembering, live in hope.

AUTUMN

All day the Planes have shaken from shadow
    to sun
Their long depending boughs, and one by one
From early-falling Limes the yellow leaves
Have eddied to earth; but still warm noon
    deceives
Our fears of change. But when with the twilight
    came
From the dim garden an air like sharp cold
    flame
And bitter with burnt leaves, I knew once more
That the walls were down between love and the
    silent, frore
Wastes of eternity. O lean above me,
Screening my eyes with your hair like a dark
    willow
From the cold glare of death. O, you that love
    me,
Lean with your body's weight, that the cold
    billow
Not yet may lift me away; though love and light,
Roses and leaves and fruit prepare to-night
With unreturning wings
To launch upon the eternal flux of things.

KENNETH H. ASHLEY

NORMAN CHURCH : NEW COALFIELD

Beneath the hill a littered landscape spread
All newly varnished by the garish sun;
New corn shone harsh and green, but new brick's
    harsher red
Showed that down there more coal than corn
    was won.
Tall chimneys flew their smoke as masts fly flags;
Great wheels on headstocks spun, and stopt, and
    spun again;
Pubs, cinemas, fried fish and chips, and fags—
Such were suggested by that cluttered plain—
Hot asphalt; Council schools; packed cottages in
    rows;
Spoil banks and cinder paths and broken hedges;
Barbed wire, corrugated iron, all that goes
With smirchèd farms and building land in wedges.
And all this litter was so raw, so new,
Even when derelicted each thing glowed,
Shattered but modern; glittered to the view
Like a smashed bottle on a tar-mac road.

The very sky, so hot, so smooth, so bright,
Seemed that day newly turned, dust-proof and
    water-tight.
And then I started; for my glance lit on
A grim grey tower, screened by foliage—
Incongruous, startling, its grey pallor shone—
A strayed spectator from another age.
I do not think I should have been
Much more surprised if I had seen
One of those men who many a year before
Had left this vale to fight at Agincourt.
If I had seen him with my eyes,
Tricked out in his forgotten guise,
Himself bewildered, but uncowed,
Pushing his way, come striding through
The gaping, staring, cloth-capped crowd,
To this old church; to this one place he knew.

COW AND SEED STACK

Thick cud riseth:
Slowly to chew—
Slowly to swallow—
Cud riseth anew.
To swing the tail—
Fly hummeth by—
Sun striketh hot:
To cover the eye.
Wind bringth a smell;
Smells well within—
To widen the nose;
Cud riseth thin.
Rare is that smell,
Rarely it puts.
Craving in belly,
Pulleth at guts.
To get me up:
To have in mind
Smelleth as that
Food that eats kind.

Slowly to rise :
To arch the back ;
To husk the throat ;
Dry joints to crack ;
So : surely to go,
Surely to find,
Food that eats well,
Up field, up wind.

GOODS TRAIN AT NIGHT

The station is empty and desolate;
A sick lamp wanly glows;
Slowly puffs a goods engine,
Slow yet alive with great energy;
Drawing rumbling truck
After rumbling, rumbling truck;
Big, half-seen, insensate.
Yet each as it jolts through the glow
Responds to the questioning light
Dumbly revealing
Diverse personality :
" Neal & Co."; " John Bugsworth "; " Nor-
    land Collieries Limited ";
" Jolly & Sons "; " Jolly & Sons "; " Jolly &
    Sons ";
Thrice repeated, percussive, insistent—
Each wet wall-side successively announcing
Names : badges and symbols of men,
Of men in their intricate trafficking—
But there quickens a deeper emotion,

Roused by the iterant names,
Beyond the mere intricate commerce,
The infinite wonder of life.
Effort and hope and love, the heart's desire,
Leap in the womb of the brain
As the trucks clang their way through the night.
Slides by the guard's van at the last,
With a last definite clatter of steel upon steel
And a glitter of ruby-red light.

So : silence recaptures the station;
The damp steam eddies out;
The drizzle weaves a silver pattern,
An endless shining silver pattern,
A silver woof in the lamplight.
And I find myself full of a grief—
A dull little grief for humanity.

THE OWL AT " THE SWAN "

You who loved twilight and the dusky night
Must perch transfixed, undazzled, in this room
Of smoke and fume and talk and garish light :
A rigid mummy in a glassy tomb,
Tawdry with paint and artificial grass,
With sand and moss, and boughs of cork and
glue,
Until some spring a careless servant lass
Shatter your case and make an end of you;
Or moth within your case finding its way
Shall breed new life to work your last decay.

You knew this countryside; your still wings were
Part of its glamour forty years ago,
As in the twilight you came sweeping there
Round stack, and ivied barn, and old hedgerow—
From Stubbins Wood you'd beat to Assarts Farm
And then by Flixter Beck to Nickerbush—
Until one eve the cool sweet curfew calm
Was broken by a gun, and with a tumbling rush

43

To earth you came; wings whirling o'er and o'er,
And life's mysterious light informed your eyes no
    more.

Your race is reckoned wise and mine more so;
But ne'er a seer of us can cast a spell,
To shield our memories safe from overthrow,
That's one whit better than your fragile shell.
And gallant bipeds, many and many a one,
Who made much stir and flutter in their day,
From their familiar hunting fields have gone,
And not one relic of their flight does stay :
Old gunning Time has ta'en them altogether,
Nor left of their brave plumage one poor feather.

PAUL BEWSHER

NOX MORTIS

The afternoon
    Flutters and dies :
The fairy moon
    Burns in the skies
As they grow darker, and the first stars shine
On Night's rich mantle—purple like warm wine.

On each white road
    Begins to crawl
The heavy toad :
    The night-birds call,
And round the trees the swift bats flit and wheel,
While from the barns the rats begin to steal.

So now must I,
    Bird of the night,
Towards the sky
    Make wheeling flight,
And bear my poison o'er the gloomy land,
And let it loose with hard unsparing hand.

The chafers boom
        With whirring wings,
And haunt the gloom
        Which twilight brings—
So in nocturnal travel do I wail
As through the night the wingèd engines sail.

Death, Grief, and Pain
        Are what I give.
O that the slain
        Might live—might live !
I know them not, for I have blindly killed,
And nameless hearts with nameless sorrow filled.

Thrice cursèd War
        Which bids that I
Such death should pour
        Down from the sky.
O, Star of Peace, rise swiftly in the East
That from such slaying men may be released.

EDMUND·BLUNDEN

BEHIND THE LINE

Treasure not so the forlorn days
When dun clouds flooded the naked plains
  With foul remorseless rains;
  Tread not those memory ways
Where by the dripping alien farms,
Starved orchards with their shrivelled arms,
The bitter mouldering wind would whine
At the brisk mules clattering towards the Line.

Remember not with so sharp skill
Each chasm in the clouds that with strange fire
  Lit pyramid-fosse and spire
  Miles on miles from our hill;
In the magic glass, aye, then their lure
Like heaven's houses gleaming pure
Might soothe the long imprisoned sight
And put the seething storm to flight.

Enact you not so like a wheel
The round of evenings in sand-bagged rooms
  Where candles flicked the glooms;
  The jests old time could steal

51

From ugly destiny, on whose brink
The poor fools grappled fear with drink,
And snubbed the hungry raving guns
With endless tunes on gramophones.

About you spreads the world anew,
The old fields all for your sense rejoice,
   Music has found her ancient voice,
   From the hills there's heaven on earth to view;
And kindly Mirth will raise his glass
To bid you with dull Care go pass—
And still you wander muttering on
Over the shades of shadows gone.

THE PASTURE POND

By the pasture pond alone
I'll call the landscape all my own,
Be the lord of all I see
From water fly to topmost tree,
And on these riches gloat this day
Till the blue mist warns away.

Here's no malice that could wither
Joy's blown flower, nor dare come hither;
No hot hurry such as drives
Men through their unsolaced lives;
Here like the bees I cannot fare
A span but find some honey there.

The small birds and great as well
In these trees and closes dwell,
And there they never grudge nor brawl
For nature gives enough for all,
Nor care crows what starling delves
Among the mole-heaps like themselves.

The thrush that haunts the mellow ground
And runs along and glances round
Will run and revel through my brain
For a blue moon befooling pain,
And elms so full of birds and song
There shall be green the winter long.

From the meadows smooth and still
Where the peewits feed their full
And into swirling rings upfly
With white breasts dazzling on the eye
To the pool itself I come
And like rapture am struck dumb :

For if fields and air are free
The water's double liberty,
Where milch cows dewlap-deep may wade
Or jack-hern ply his cunning trade—
Else what but vision dares intrude
That many peopled solitude?

The astonished clouds seem lingering here
For dragon-flies so whip and veer
And take the sun and turn to flame
They'd make the fastest cloud seem lame,
Or breaths of wind that sometimes fly
And cut faint furrows and are by.

So well may I admire the pool
Where thistles and their caps of wool
(Whence those sly winds some flecks purloin)
Stand sentinels at every coign,
And sorrels rusty-red have banned
Each place the thistle left unmanned.

But passing through, an old ally,
Into the bright deeps I may spy,
Where merry younkers, roach or rudd,
Jump for the fly and flounce and scud;
That care for no one now, and live
For every pleasure pools can give.

In russet weeds, by the sunken boat,
That grudge each other room to float,
They hide along, grown fine and fat,
I hear them like a lapping cat
Feed from the stems till hunger's done—
Then out agen to find the sun.

The moorhen, too, as proud as they
With jerking neck is making way
In horse-shoe creeks where old pike rest
And beetles skate in jostling jest;
And overhead as large as wrens
Dance hobby-horses of the fens—

From all these happy folk I find
Life's radiance kindled in my mind,
And even when homeward last I turn
How bright the hawthorn berries burn,
How steady in the old elm still
The great woodpecker strikes his bill;

Whose labour oft in vain is given,
Yet never he upbraids high heaven;
Such trust is his. O I have heard
No sweeter from a singing bird
Than his tap-tapping there this day,
That said what words will never say.

The bells from humble steeples call,
Nor will I be the last of all
To pass between the ringers strong
And as of old make evensong;
While over pond and plat and hall
The first of sleep begins to fall.

Time, like an ever rolling stream!
Through the yew the sun's last gleam
Lights into a glory extreme
The squirrel carven pews that dream
Of my fathers far beyond
Their solitary pasture-pond.

THE SCYTHE STRUCK BY LIGHTNING

A thick hot haze had choked the valley grounds
Long since, the dogday sun had gone his rounds
Like a dull coal half lit with sulky heat;
And leas were iron, ponds were clay, fierce beat
The blackening flies round moody cattle's eyes.
Wasps on the mudbank seemed a hornet's size
That on the dead roach battened. The plough's
    increase
Stood under a curse.

      Behold, the far release !
Old wisdom breathless at her cottage door
" Sounds of abundance " mused, and heard the
    roar
Of marshalled armies in the silent air,
And thought Elisha stood beside her there,
And clacking reckoned ere the next nightfall
She'd turn the looking-glasses to the wall.

Faster than armies out of the burnt void
The hour-glass clouds innumerably deployed,

And when the hay-folks next look up, the sky
Sags black above them; scarce is time to fly.
And most run for their cottages; but Ward,
The mower for the inn beside the ford,
And slow strides he with shouldered scythe still
    bare,
While to the coverts leaps the great-eyed hare.
As he came in the dust snatched up and whirled
Hung high, and like a bell-rope whipped and
    twirled;
The blazen light glared round, the haze resolved
Into demoniac shapes bulged and convolved.
Well might poor ewes afar make bleatings wild,
Though this old trusting mower sat and smiled,
For from the hush of many days the land
Had waked itself : and now on every hand
Shrill swift alarm notes, cries and counter-cries,
Lowings and crowings came and throbbing sighs.
Now atom lightning brandished on the moor,
Then out of sullen drumming came the roar
Of thunder joining east and west :
In hedge and orchard small birds durst not rest,
Flittering like dead leaves and like wisps of
    straws,
And the cuckoo called again, for without pause

Oncoming voices in the vortex burred.
The storm came toppling like a wave, and blurred
In grey the trees that like black steeples towered.
The sun's last yellow died.   Then who but
    cowered ?
Down ruddying darkness floods the hideous flash,
And pole to pole the cataract whirlwinds clash.

Alone within the tavern parlour still
Sat the grey mower, pondering on God's will,
And flinching not to flame or bolt, that swooped
With a great hissing rain till terror drooped
In weariness : and then there came a roar
Ten-thousand-fold, he saw not, was no more—
But life bursts on him once again, and blood
Beats droning round, and light comes in a flood.

He stares, and sees the sashes battered awry,
The wainscot shivered, the crocks shattered, and
    by,
His twisted scythe, melted by its fierce foe,
Whose Parthian shot struck down the chimney.
    Slow
Old Ward lays hand to his old working-friend,
And thanking God Whose mercy did defend

His servant, yet must drop a tear or two
And think of times when that old scythe was new,
And stands in silent grief, nor hears the voices
Of many a bird that through the lands rejoices,
Nor sees through the smashed panes the seagreen
    sky,
That ripens into blue, nor knows the storm is by.

THE POOR MAN'S PIG

Already fallen plum-bloom stars the green
And apple-boughs as knarred as old toads' backs
Wear their small roses ere a rose is seen;
  The building thrush watches old Job who
      stacks
The bright-peeled osiers on the sunny fence,
  The pent sow grunts to hear him stumping by,
And tries to push the bolt and scamper thence,
  But her ringed snout still keeps her to the sty.

Then out he lets her run; away she snorts
  In bundling gallop for the cottage door,
With hungry hubbub begging crusts and orts,
  Then like a whirlwind bumping round once
      more;
Nuzzling the dog, making the pullets run,
  And sulky as a child when her play's done.

OLD HOMES

O happiest village, how I turned to you,
Beyond estranging years that cloaked my view
With all their heavy fogs of fear and pain;
I turned to you, and never turned in vain.
Through fields yet ringing sad with fancy's dirge,
Landscapes that hunt poor sleep to bedlam's
    verge,
Green glow your leas, and sweet resound your
    woods,
And there is laughter in your summer floods.

There the old houses where we lived abide,
And I shall see them, though hot tears should
    hide
The ken of " home " from that which now I hold.
What though pulled down?—to me they're as of
    old.
Those garrets creak as I tiptoe the boards
To find the last lone tenant's fabled hoards,
And silver on the dun November sky
Through quaking panes I see the flood race by

Brown hilltops where the black bines moulder out.
To those same panes when full moon comes about
I hastening home lift daring eyes to learn
If ghost eyes through their sullen crystal burn,
And feel what sight cannot report, and fall
A-shuddering even to face the unlit hall.

Passages crooked and slanted, ceilings stooped,
And yews with drowsy arras overdrooped
The windows of that home, the broad hearths
    wept
With every shower; a-dry the great vats slept,
Where one time kercher'd maids had toiled with
    a will;
Such nooks were here, a hundred scarce would
    fill.
And in the farm beside, the barn's sunk tiles
Enclosed a space like to the church's aisles.

Then all about those vasty halls our play
Would hold the evening's lanterned gloom at bay,
And senses young received each new-found thing
As meadows feel and glow with eager spring :
Thence we have journeyed out to the blue hills
    round,
The pilgrims of a day's enchanted ground,

And where we'd seen the crow or heron fly
Have made our foreign way, passed far inns by,
On edge of lily ponds have heard the jack
From unknown holes leap and shrunk trembling
    back,
Have seen strange chimneys smoke, new runnels
    foam,
Until quite surfeited we turned for home,
Whose white walls rosy with the westering light
Still of our journey seemed the noblest sight.

Thence, too, when high wind through the black
    clouds pouring
Bowing the strong trees' creaking joints went
    roaring,
Adventure was to splash through the sightless
    lane
When church bells filled a pause of wind and rain,
And once within the venerable walls
To hear the elms without like waterfalls,
While the cold arches murmured every prayer,
And Advent hymns bade the round world pre-
    pare,
Prepare ! the next day with pale seas amazed,
We scarce had marvelled as we gaped and gazed,

If this had been the tempest harbinger
Of the world's end and final Arbiter :
The pollards in the yellow torrent drowning,
The weir's huge jaw a-gnashing, all heaven
      frowning.

But there at length, beside that thunderous weir,
Our lot was cast, and no less generous here
Came each long day; not even the hours we spent
Under the dominie's eye unkindly went.
We found his learning dry, 'tis true, and hit
Disaster in our sleights for leavening it;
But the old desks cut with heroic names,
The gilded panel trumpeting past fames,
Shields, pictures, solemn books of stars and sages
Kindled our pride in sense of mightier ages,
That old school now will never see again.
Fair, fair befall her, though no urchin pen
Crawl through the summer hours beneath her
      beams,
Nor playground roystering shout bestir her
      dreams,
Honoured among her aspens may she rise,
And her red walls long soothe the traveller's eyes.
Thence issued we among the scampering crew,
And crossed the green, and from the bridge down
      threw

Our dinner crumbs to waiting roach; or soft
Marauding climbed the cobwebbed apple loft,
And the sweet smell of blenheims lapped in straw
Made stolen pleasure seem a natural law;
Escape and plunder hurried us at last
To the lock cottage where our lot was cast,
Poor as church mice, yet rich at every turn,
Who never guessed that man was made to mourn.

In this same country as the time fulfilled,
When hops like ribbons on the maypole frilled
Their colonnaded props mile after mile,
And tattered armies gathered to the spoil,
We, too, invaders the green arbours ere
The day had glistened on earth's dewy hair,
And through the heat we picked and picked
    apace,
To fill our half bin and not lose the chace,
While our bin partner, fierce of eye and tongue,
Minded our ways and gave " when I was
    young ";
And all about, the clearing setts revealed
The curious colours of the folk afield,
The raven hair, the flamy silk, the blue
Washed purple with all weathers; crime's dark
    crew;

Babes at the breast; old sailors chewing quids;
And hyacinth eyes beneath sweet country lids.
The conquest sped, the bramblings, goldings small,
The heavy fuggles to the bins came all,
Garden past garden heard the measurer's horn
Blow truce, advance! until a chillier morn
Saw the last wain load up with pokes and go,
And an empty, saddened field looked out below
On trees where kindled the quick feverous tinge
Of autumn, and the river's glaucous fringe,
And our own cottage, its far lattice twinkling
Across the tired stubble sown with sheepbells'
    tinkling
On airy wings the warning spirit sighed,
But we, we heard not, thinking of Christmastide.

A love I had, as childhood ever will,
And our first meeting I'll remember still;
When to the farmhouse first we went, the may
With white and red lit hedgerows all the way,
And there I saw her in a red-may cloak,
To church going by; so delicate she spoke,
So graceful stept, so innocent-gay was her look,
I took a flower; she put it in her book,
And after many eves we've walked for hours
Like loving flowers among the other flowers,

And blushed for pride when other girls and boys
Laughed at us sweethearts in the playhour's
 noise—
Sweethearts, it was a silly simple thing,
And we've gone each our ways this many a
 spring,
But now to see the child with child primrosing
Is all as sweet as any spring's unclosing.

Vision on vision blooms—long may they bloom,
Through years that bring the philosophic gloom,
Sweetening my sleep with its strange agonies
 racked
And shedding dew on every parching tract.
In every pleasant place a virtue adding,
A herb of grace to keep the will from madding :
And, happiest village, still I turn to you,
The alabaster box of spikenard, you;
To your knoll trees, your slow canal return,
In your kind farms or cottages sojourn ;
Enjoy the whim that on your church tower set
The lead cowl like a Turkish minaret ;
Beat all your bounds, record each kiln and shed,
And see the blue mists on each calm close spread.
My day still breaks beyond your poplared East,
And in your pastoral still my life has rest.

PERCH-FISHING

On the far hill the cloud of thunder grew
And sunlight blurred below; but sultry blue
Burned yet on the valley water where it hoards
Behind the miller's elmen floodgate boards,
And there the wasps, that lodge them ill-
    concealed
In the vole's empty house, still drove afield
To plunder touchwood from old crippled trees
And build their young ones their hutched
    nurseries;
Still creaked the grasshoppers' rasping unison
Nor had the whisper through the tansies run
Nor weather-wisest bird gone home.

                    How then
Should wry eels in the pebbled shallows ken
Lightning coming? Troubled up they stole
To the deep-shadowed sullen water-hole,
Among whose warty snags the quaint perch lair.
As cunning stole the boys to angle there,

Muffling least tread, with no noise balancing
    through
The hangdog alder-boughs his bright bamboo.
Down plumbed the shuttled ledger, and the quill
On the quicksilver water lay dead still.

A sharp snatch, swirling to-fro of the line,
He's lost, he's won, with splash and scuffling
    shine
Past the low-lapping brandy-flowers drawn in,
The ogling hunchback perch with needled fin.
And there beside him one as large as he,
Following his hooked mate, careless who shall see
Or what befall him, close and closer yet—
The startled boy might take him in his net
That folds the other.

                  Slow, while on the clay
The other flounces, slow he sinks away.
What agony usurps that watery brain
For comradeship of twenty summers slain,
For such delights below the flashing weir
And up the sluice-cut, playing buccaneer
Among the minnows; lolling in hot sun
When bathing vagabonds had drest and done;

Rootling in salty flannel-weed for meal
And river shrimps, when hushed the trundling
 wheel;
Snapping the dapping moth, and with new
 wonder
Prowling through old drowned barges falling
 asunder.
And O a thousand things the whole year through
They did together, never more to do.

THE CHILD'S GRAVE

I came to the churchyard where pretty Joy lies
  On a morning in April, a rare sunny day;
Such bloom rose around, and so many birds' cries
  That I sang for delight as I followed the way.

I sang for delight in the ripening of spring,
  For dandelions even were suns come to earth;
Not a moment went by but a new lark took wing
  To wait on the season with melody's mirth.

Love-making birds were my mates all the road,
  And who would wish surer delight for the eye
Than to see pairing goldfinches gleaming abroad
  Or yellowhammers sunning on paling and sty?

And stocks in the almswomen's garden were
    blown,
  With rich Easter roses each side of the door;
The lazy white owls in the glade cool and lone
  Paid calls on their cousins in the elm's cham-
    bered core.

72

This peace, then, and happiness thronged me
    around.
  Nor could I go burdened with grief, but made
    merry
Till I came to the gate of that overgrown ground
  Where scarce once a year sees the priest come
    to bury.

Over the mounds stood the nettles in pride,
  And, where no fine flowers, there kind weeds
    dared to wave;
It seemed but as yesterday she lay by my side,
  And now my dog ate of the grass on her grave.

He licked my hand wondering to see me muse so,
  And wished I would lead on the journey or
    home,
As though not a moment of spring were to go
  In brooding; but I stood, if her spirit might
    come

And tell me her life, since we left her that day
  In the white lilied coffin, and rained down our
    tears;

But the grave held no answer, though long I
    should stay;
  How strange that this clay should mingle with
    hers!

So I called my good dog, and went on my way;
  Joy's spirit shone then in each flower I went by,
And clear as the noon, in coppice and ley,
  Her sweet dawning smile and her violet eye!

FREDERICK V. BRANFORD

FREDERICK V. BRANFORD

SECRET TREATIES

We thought to find a cross like Calvary's,
And queened proud England with a diadem
Of thorns. Impetuous armies clamouring
For war, from the far utterance of the seas
We sprang, to win a new Jerusalem.
Now is our shame, for we have seen you fling
Full-sounding honour from your lips like phlegm
And bargain up our soul in felonies.

O England, it were better men should read,
In dusty chronicles, of how a death
Had found thee in the van of these crusades;
To tell their eager sons with bated breath,
And burning eyes, about a golden deed,
A vanished race, and high immortal Shades.

FREDERICK V. BRANFORD

NIGHT FLYING

Aloft on footless levels of the night
A pilot thunders through the desolate stars,
Sees in the misty deep a fainting light
Of far-off cities cast in coal-dark bars
Of shore and soundless sea; and he is lone,
Snatched from the universe like one forbid,
Or like a ghost caught from the clay and thrown
Out on the void, nor God cared what he did.

Till from these unlinked whisperers that pain
The buried earth he swings his boat away,
Even as a lonely thinker who hath run
The gamut of great lore, and found the Inane,
Then stumbles at midnight upon a sun
And all the honour of a mighty day.

OVER THE DEAD

Who in the splendour of a simple thought,
Whether for England or her enemies,
Went in the night, and in the morning died;
Each bleeding piece of human earth that lies
Stark to the carrion wind, and groaning cries
For burial—each Jesu crucified—
Hath surely won the thing He dearly bought;
For wrong is right when wrong is greatly wrought.

Yet is the Nazarene no thane of Thor,
To play on partial fields the puppet king,
Bearing the battle down with bloody hand.
Serene he stands, above the gods of war,
A naked man where shells go thundering—
The great unchallenged Lord of No-Man's Land.

THE DÆMON

Pit-a-pat, pit-a-pat,
All the dark years I never heard that
Pit-a-pat, pit-a-pat.

When I stood
In the black wood
    Apart,
Where the swarm
Of devils storm
With a worm
In my heart.
Pit-a-pat.
I never heard that.

Pit-a-pat, pit-a-pat,
    Twenty-three winters,
    All icicle splinters.
    Twenty-three springs,
    All green ghast stings.

Twenty-three autumns
Twirled like teetotums,
Twenty-three summers,
Mouthing like mummers,
Hustled and hurled,
World within world.
Pit-a-pat, pit-a-pat.
All the dark years I never heard that.

Pit-a-pat, pit-a-pat.
At dead midnight,
Like the spirit of fright
When I stood on the brink
Of Hell—I think
I should have gone mad
If not for the glad,
Soft silence of that
Pit-a-pat, pit-a-pat.

The protean churl,
Like a passionate girl,
Came to the tip
Of my heart with a lip
So slight, that it seemed
As though I had dreamed

81

Then away fled he
Into mystery.
Pit-a-pat.
Two dark years I never heard that.

Pit-a-pat, pit-a-pat.
Yester year I again heard that,
    Louder and longer,
    Prouder and stronger
    He came, with the beat
    Of storms in his feet;
    Came with the flash
    Of lightning, the crash
    Of planets under
    Shattering thunder.
    I felt the dart
    Of his tongue to my heart,
    The flaming bands
    Of his iron hands
    Tearing the ghost
    Of my will from his post.
    He slaked me my drouth
    In the wine of his mouth,
    Flooding a red
    Foam through my head,

So that I stood,
Like a man made of blood
In a drunken daze,
Singing his praise.

Pit-a-pat, pit-a-pat.
Yester-night I again heard that.
Clear and sure.
I flung the door.
    In trod
      The god.

He held a glass
Where all time was.
He took the sands
In his hands,
And let them pour
Upon the floor.
He bid me tell
Them as they fell.

I counted once,
I counted twice;
He said, " O dunce,
Count thou them thrice."

In a trice
I counted thrice

'As the sand
Slipped through his hand;
I counted seven separate times
The sands in seven separate rhymes.
But how often I might count
I always made a strange amount,
For the sands would always run
Out of numbers into None.

Then he caught a million miles,
And set them on the floor in piles
And he caught a million others
And set them down beside their brothers
He took so many million more
That all space lay on the floor.

He bid me tell the miles, but I,
Howsoever I might try,
Found, as I had found before,
Always Nothing on the floor.

Then he took a million men,
A million others, and again
Million upon million hurled,
Till all the nations of the world
Were in my little chamber, even
All the denizens of heaven.

Thus he laboured to rehearse
The pageant of the Universe,
And ever at each total beauty
He bid me do my ghastly duty.
But howsoever I might count,
I always made that strange amount,
Till I heard the Dæmon cry,
" The whole is here, and it is I."

Then I looked long, long at him,
Till I grew faint and very dim.
And I saw to my surprise
My spirit standing in his eyes.
And I saw a symbol sit,
Awful, on the head of it.
I saw a dread, unspoken truth
(Dare I say it, in my youth,
When I have yet some days perchance
To mingle with earth's circumstance?).
I saw—I saw—O God!—I saw
(Speak it low with holy awe,
Speak it difficult and dark,
Lest the sons of Adam hark),
That I, two thousand years, had worn
On Calvary, the Crown of Thorn.

A. Y. CAMPBELL

SOLUS HYPERBOREAS

(May, 1915)

Ode to a pocket edition of Virgil in the possession of D. G. Lillie, biologist to the British Antarctic Expedition, 1910.

(Note.—The volcano Erebus was within sight of the base camp.)

Much-travelled, curious book, I write this
    reverent ode
  To celebrate thy fame, and praise thy loving
      carrier;
That thou wast Virgil, always a most precious
    load,
Now doubly wonderful, secure in safe abode,
  First of all Virgils to have reached the Great
     Ice Barrier.

There, like thine Orpheus, didst thou the lone
    realm enchant,

Thrilling eternal snows with song unprece-
dented;
There saw'st an Erebus more grim and gaunt
Than that whose gloomy king
Wept and relented,
Hearing but once the Thracian minstrel sing,
And the remorseless powers of sightless Death
repented.
A desert even for shades too bare
Was that thy presence graced,
Pinnacled with a skyey gorge
That fumes like the Sicilian forge—
But what man's bleak imagination dare
With snowy Cyclops haunt the inhuman waste,
Or in that frost-bound Ætna dream some
Typhon's lair?

Yet 'twere a grievous error
To think that here no forms are seen or heard.
The subtle force of Life is not so soon deterred,
And even the glittering shores of Erebus and
Terror,
Untenanted and rigid as they seem,
Harbour a countless herd
Of beast, fish, bird, that their own shelters
mock
Or lurk in blinding gleam;

And silver sea, white landscape, and black rock
  With undetected animation teem.
Nor is a land for half the year benighted,
  A trackless and immeasurable wold
    By marrow-piercing cold
And barrenness so desperately blighted
    But thou didst there behold
Creatures in which thy lord would have de-
      lighted—
Nay, which his inward vision long ago had
      sighted.

Thou didst see Proteus there, and his am-
      phibious flock
  Of soft-eyed seals disporting on the beach,
Either lumbering along from rock to rock,
  Or blissfully rotating each
In his particular marble dock,
Or in its brittle walls laborious channels hollow-
      ing.
Thou didst see Phorcus and his playful following
  Of huge cetaceans
Riding along the waves, tumbling and wallowing,
  And tracedst their luxurious gyrations
    By their high-snorted fountains.
  Thou hast seen penguins, too, their populous
      nations

Blackening the distant mountains,
Or near at hand hast watched their congregations
Flickering with movement, filled with clamours
raucous,
Or thou hast heard a small loquacious knot
On icy crag some raid or rapine plot
In squabbling conclave or intriguing caucus.
And thou mayst even have snatched, in some
remoter spot
Like a sea-lion couchant in stalactite grot,
A fleeting glimpse of Glaucus.

But fitly to rehearse
And with full circumstance unfold each miracle
Were difficult in this exacting verse
And far too long a task for measures lyrical.
Nay, it would need thy master's happy skill,
And a fifth Georgic fill,
In some such playful-epic vein
And in such human image to describe
With grandiose-tender strain
The wondrous commune of the penguin tribe.
The civil code which they from birth imbibe,

Their ritual, fasts, and games,
  " A world in little, yet a vision rare,"*
Their hymeneal bliss, which our own conduct
    shames,
  Their inexhaustible parental care,
And all the complex laws of their small lives,
  His were the mind most proper to declare
Who voiced the marvels of our humble hives,
  And the minute society of bees laid bare.

  All Nature's works he saw
  With wonder, love, and awe,
And might have used his humour mixed with
    pity
  To illuminate and draw
The charm and pathos of that Polar city,
  And those quaint colonists of ice and wave,
Who, in a world with circling perils rife,
  Their pygmy species to eternise, brave
The elements themselves in constant strife,
And mid perpetual cold preserve the fire of life.

But thou henceforth shalt tell a double tale :
One, of that patriarchal navigator
  Who from the flames of Pergamum set sail,
  Destined old wonders of the deep to probe ;

* Georg., iv. 3 : Admiranda tibi levium spectacula rerum.

This shall men read in the familiar lines
Of which thou art the small perpetuator.
  But thou hast other speaking signs
    In blots and blurs that stain thy weathered
      robe,
Whether of sportive baptism at the Equator,
  Or caught in some Antarctic gale
    Where seas, unreined by continents, roll
      round the globe.
And in these characters the skilled translator
  May read another tale
  Rich in romance no less, vaster in scale;
    A voyage of enterprise heroic,
  As full of purpose high,
    Labour indomitable, and courage Stoic,
And no less sure than that, of immortality.

So, when thy future readers shall discover
  How, in that hospitable land,
His first long phase of storm and struggle over,
  The weather-beaten Trojan scanned,
    Far from his ancient home, in their out-
      landish art,
Scenes of old war, and sad imperishable glories;
  The vision stirred his heart,
    He cried : " Here, too, are tears; here, too,
      compassion "—

Then shall they pause, and fashion
Another story's deathless record to thy story's,
    And their proud hearts shall beat,
    While they with reverence the great line repeat,
Quae regio in terris nostri non plena laboris?

Yes, regions where no conquering Roman ever
        stepped
    To man's invincibility redound;
Where, in white leagues of snowdrift blizzard-
        swept,
    A solitary mound
      Through the long Polar nights unvisited,
Where that last sleep they slept,
    Commemorates their labours and our loss;
There men once wept;
      There too, there tears were shed;
    There, symbol of compassion, stands a simple
        Cross.

Yet not the lands they gained, nor the funereal
        Pole
    They reached, alas too late, their triumph sum;
It was no popular feat that was their goal,
    But to make tameless Scythian tracts become

The provinces of Knowledge; to unroll
Nature's Sibylline scroll,
　　Teach mysteries to speak that had been dumb,
And to promote the bounds of man's imperial
　　　　soul.

　　And this was their achievement;
Here they annexed and charted an immense
　　　　domain,
For their own memories a greater gain,
　　For us, a better solace in bereavement
Than that priority which they did not attain.
　　And surely of all men he
　　Whose art created thee,
If to thy pages he his heart committed,
　　And truly held that man most fortunate
　　　　Who to the secret springs
　　　　And causes of all things
　　Had skill to penetrate,
Would count them to be envied and not pitied.

　　Happy is he indeed,
Happier than vulgar minds can ever grasp,
Who chose the book of Knowledge to unclasp,
　　And her high doctrines read;
　　Filled with a faith more large than any creed
By the harmonious spectacle of Science,

Awed but not cowed,
He finds in Truth alone his light and lead,
And to her service vowed
Bids Superstition, Fear, and Fate, and Death,
defiance.

Such faith enjoys the man who treasured thee.
Yet is he doubly blest,
Being dowered in like degree
With what thou dost attest
To have been in Virgil's mind the next felicity.
His devious foot ere now hath pressed
The grassy shrine of many a rural god;
Of wood-nymphs' arbours he hath been a ranger,
And in Silvanus' precincts trod,
Nor is elusive Pan to him a stranger,
For he loves peace no less than he dares danger.

These are the two ideals at whose leading
He now goes forth, not to destroy, but heal;
And, because thousands of brave men are bleed-
ing,
To face that death which he would never deal,
All his most cherished labours has relinquished.

May he survive till Europe shall resume
Those noble quests that now have been extin-
    guished,
    And that devotion use, which wasteful wars
      consume.

But thou, henceforth on thy twin laurels rest;
    And let thy thumbed and venerable pages
    Stand silent monitors to future ages
Of what alone can make man truly great and
    blest.

To spread the power of learning, and the light of
    art,
    Further than sage or poet ever dreamed,
      To leave not yet unfurled
No corner of Earth's chart,
    No nation of her millions unredeemed;
      But like that box which dying Douglas
      hurled
Charged with his cause and his great leader's
    heart,
    Far, far ahead of our own vital span
      To fling Regeneration at the world—
This is the glory, this the work, of man;
And of this progress thou, small book, wast in the
    van.

IN A WARM OCTOBER

Only a memory is the lilac now;
  The nightingale not even a memory.
  Two months, three months back, did the
    cuckoo fly;
One month before that took his Trappist vow.
Gone are the swallows even, when? whither?
    how?
  Yet one great rich rose blazes garishly;
And once more crawls the meditative plough;
  And still the suns soar cloudless, hot, and high.

Glad though not thrilled I walk, even as the year;
  See little, think little, blink, feel the sun.
Birds there may be yet, none I care to hear;
  Hopes I may nurse, but would not mention
    one.
What still is with me, I reflect how dear;
  If I have lost some things, their thought I shun.

THERE ARE STILL KINGFISHERS

Faith peace and joy to-day brings; all has failed
I this day put my hand to, well know I;
Less blind than some so far, though that's not
    why;
But with joy peace and faith my spirit is mailed,
Since on Wren's bridge at noon, unseen, unhailed,
I, all alone, saw the kingfisher fly.

Not as before, startled by friendly prod,
In stagnant ditch to imagine something quiver,
Lost while half-seen; but brilliant, clear, and
    broad,
Forty-two yards up the middle of the river
Under my eyes shot the turquoise unflawed!
Nothing of me that bird knows and will never;
But I rejoiced, as men rejoice in God,
Not that he cares for them, but lives forever.

28th APRIL, 1917

Hush, hush, inhuman one! Haunt moonlit
    arbours;
  Revel; ay, love; but noiseless; never sing!
Hast thou no sense what heart of listener
    harbours?
  Oh, is this Spring to thee no less than Spring?

I heard thee suddenly; that ancient impulse
  Breathless to hearken, seized me unaware,
Even as I heard of old, and felt the dim pulse
  Of Earth speak through thee, and thy bliss
    could share.

Now, what a pang it brought, the rapture
    piercing!
  Hast thou no heart? Thou, that in years now
    fled
So sang, that in thy voice we seemed to hear
    sing
  Our hearts—in days before our friends were
    dead.

How canst thou come again, true to thy season,
   Woo, mate, make music, as when Spring was
      joy?
How canst thou sing to us without a reason?
   Must thou our dear-bought calm of mind
      destroy?

We could endure the flowers; though memories
      tragic
   With their soft beauty woke, it lulled our pain.
Thou hast a soul, and with resistless magic
   Whisperest of hopes we dare not nurse again.

Till we can hear thee as these blithe new-comers,
   Cuckoos and swallows, that make no heart sore,
Cease; for our children there shall still be
      summers;
   Thou'lt sing for them so, though for us no
      more.

If thou canst feel, then, wait till we are older;
   Wiser; to loss resigned; the way less long.
Dreams, and strange hopes that rise, desires
      grown bolder,
   Old mystic thoughts revived, rare glints of
      song—

These wouldst thou bring us now, but old friends
    bring not?
  O, for one year yet, shun thy wonted grove;
Or visit us as thou didst once, but sing not;
  Or sing, O nightingale, but not of love.

A. Y. CAMPBELL.

EXILED FROM THE NIGHTINGALES

Now that soft April steals the voice,
  The garb of May, the scented air,
Where last spring saw me men rejoice;
  And I rejoice too, though not there.

The lawns I miss, they miss not me,
  Their freshness must be still the same;
And in those groves I may not see
  Still sings the bird I dare not name.

ON THE BIRTH OF ADRIAN

A child is born, unborn before;
   A male child; let the world rejoice.
Leap, town and country, dale and shore;
   And thou too, Muse, renew thy voice.

Born is to-day for Man fresh hope,
   Born of redemption one more sign;
Born is for all unborn such scope
   As none born earlier dares define.

One beast is as another beast;
   In dawns if we some difference scan,
The same sun soars in the same East,
   But one man is no other man.

Song-birds, the pride of flower and leaf,
   True is their function to its day,
Beautiful is their prime and brief;
   But one man's work shall last for aye.

Sweet is the love of womankind;
  In her pure heart, let empires fall,
One his one sure delight shall find;
  But one man's acts shall profit all.

See ye the lilies of the field?
  They toil not, neither do they spin.
A thing that pen or spear shall wield
  To sweat and rage see here begin.

See ye the lilies of the soil?
  Solomon, girt with bended knees,
Robed in all hues of human toil,
  Was not arrayed like one of these.

But wisdom, justice, knowledge, art,
  Woven into lore that shall not fail,
There lies Creation's human part,
  And stern adornment of the male.

Splendour there is of Intellect;
  It is Man's empire; here alone
Nature, in all her glory decked,
  Weighs not one thought of Solomon.

A. Y. CAMPBELL

ON THE THIRD BIRTHDAY OF STELLA

Little, fiery, twinkling thing,
　In my heaven I find thee;
Seen but as a glittering,
　Yet a world's behind thee.

Ere thou dawnedst, a new star,
　How long lurked thy traces?
Sped thy tiny beam how far
　Through the heavenly spaces?

New-born wast thou; but how old?
　Who, when, wherefore set thee
Where thou must be years untold
　Ere our night should get thee?

Not from us two, moon and sun,
　Shines thy light dependent;
Thou no planet art, but one
　Of the fixed resplendent.

A. Y. CAMPBELL

Fondly through refracting hope
  I with far conjecture
Scan, as in a telescope,
  Thy whole future's picture.

Little fiery twinkling thing,
  Easier 'twas to find thee
Than from thy shy glittering
  Guess what rolls behind thee.

ENVOI

Off, little seeds, on Time's wild gale!
  Small, but well-armoured, light yet strong.
Groan not, as through much chaff you sail;
  In seeds, remember, life sleeps long.

Some but for wind might strike root now;
  Most from the rocks will drink no tears;
Few will arrive, somewhen or how;
  But none yet for a hundred years.

DUDLEY CAREW

THE WANDERER

All things are called to home when day is done
And Mind, the Mother, standing by the door
Calls to her children who have loved the sun
But leave their play and look to him no more.

One only does not answer. One still plays
And climbs the highest boughs of topmost trees,
Sees the funereal panoply of days
And drowns his heart in depths of evening seas.

Heaven has courtiers true to dying kings.
The clouds of sunset fall in his embrace
And fold about his death their golden wings
And no more shall the Mother see one face.

GWEN CLEAR

FIDDLE SONG

Some times beside a violin I stand,
And look from the fine fiddle to my hand
And back again where potent music lies
Pent up within its technicalities.
Music's quiescence mocks me where I stand,
Silent, beside its mute intricacies.

There are three friends, and two know not each
    other.
The Soul stands whispering sweetly—" Sister . . .
    Brother . . .
The World's unuttered music hides within ". . .
And yet the hand knows not the violin.

GRIEF

Grief moves not,
She is stunned;
Nor murmurs,
She is dumb
And impotent to sound.
Great Michael, should he come
In flame, could not assail
The impenetrable veil
Of peace that wraps her round.
Grief hath no bitterness,
Nor vaunteth her distress;
Grief weeps not—
She is spent
With disillusionment;
Knowing not tide, nor time, nor high event.

Grief heareth not at all;
Is deaf to every call
From those forgotten lands
Whence Life came with full hands.

She hath no part or portion with rich earth,
Being foredoomed to suffer endless dearth
In the strange wastes where Beauty hath no
    birth.
Like windows barred at night,
Her eyes do hold no light,
And shed no rays without.
Perforce, who goeth by,
Knocking for lights, must cry—
" Their candles are all out."

PADRAIC COLUM

THE DEER OF IRELAND

An old man said, " I saw
The chief of the things that are gone;
A stag with head held high,
A doe, and a fawn;

" And they were the deer of Ireland
That scorned to breed within bound :
The last; they left no race
Tame on a pleasure ground.

" A stag, with his hide all rough
With the dew, and a doe and a fawn;
Nearby, on their track on the mountain
I watched them, two and one,

" Down to the Shannon going—
Did its waters cease to flow,
When they passed, they that carried the swift-
    ness,
And the pride of long ago?

" The last of the troop that had heard
Finn's and Oscar's cry;
A doe and a fawn, and before,
A stag with head held high ! "

FRANCES CORNFORD

SUSAN TO DIANA

A VILLANELLE

Your youth is like a water-wetted stone,
A pebble by the living sea made rare,
Bright with a beauty that is not its own.

Behold it flushed like flowers newly-blown,
Miraculously fresh beyond compare—
Your youth is like a water-wetted stone.

For when the triumphing tide recedes, alone
The stone will stay, and shine no longer there
Bright with a beauty that is not its own.

But lie and dry as joyless as a bone,
Because the sorceress sea has gone elsewhere.
Your youth is like a water-wetted stone.

Then all your lovers will be children, shown
Their treasure only transitory-fair,
Bright with a beauty that is not its own.

Remember this before your hour is flown;
O you, who are so glorious, beware!
Your youth is like a water-wetted stone,
Bright with a beauty that is not its own.

RHYME FOR A PHONETICIAN

Brave English language, you are strong as trees,
Yet intricate and stately—Thus one sees
Through branches clear-embroidered stars. You
    please
Our sense as damask roses on the breeze,
And barns that smell of hay, and bread and
    cheese.
Rustic yet Roman—yours are dignities
Sonorous as the sea's sound. On my knees
I would give thanks for all your words. Yet
    these—
Our legacy and our delight—he'd squeeze
And nip and dock and drill, to write with ease
Comershul memoz faw the Pawchoogcese.

THE HILLS

Out of the complicated house, come I
To walk beneath the sky.
Here mud and stones and turf, here everything
Is mutely comforting.
Now hung upon the twigs than thorns appear
A host of lovely rain-drops cold and clear.
And on the bank
Or deep in brambly hedges dank
The small birds nip about, and say :
" Brothers, the Spring is not so far away ! "
The hills like mother-giantesses old
Lie in the cold.
And with a complete patience, let
The cows come cropping on their bosoms wet,
And even tolerate that such as I
Should wander by
With paltry leathern heel which cannot harm
Their bodies calm ;
And, with a heart they cannot know, to bless
The enormous power of their peacefulness.

E   129

OUT OF DOORS

Lie down O woman, let the September sun
Pour with huge bounty on your bleachèd skin,
The little, last, remaining spiders run
From the dry leaves about your fingers thin.

Heed not, O Sun, her cares or her desires;
Renew her body, let her spirit pass
Into the spirit of the autumn fires,
Far noises, mountains, and the stalks of grass.

EDWARD DAVISON

I HEARD THE OLD MEN

*(Lines on being told that I had all the illusions
of youth.)*

I heard the old men talk together,
Nodding grey heads one to another,
And dimly seen from my window-sill
(So cool was dusk and the air so still)
The blue tobacco-cloud under me
Blossomed up from the vanishing tree
Till darkness gathered the phantom flower.
But under the leafage hour by hour
One to another I heard them say
Yesterday—Yesterday—Yesterday!
    *   *   *   *

It is all true that men born long ago
Pondered and spoke even as I do now,
Planning to mend earth's sorrows : even so
Do I. With earnest voice and serious brow
Each learned life's lurking secrets from the wise,
Like me they loved, growing old in discontent,
Till all illusion faded from their eyes ;
Beauty's mirage, brief and impermanent,

And first love's all-too-soon frustrated dream,
And impulse mocked and hope and faith belied,
All that was highest in the heart's esteem
Betrayed, exhausted, hurt, unsatisfied.

It is not all a dream, though when I speak
The old men smile and cowardice defers;
Ambition, Hope and Love seem strangely weak
And perishable things,—poor travellers
Treading an alien land where the sea-mark
Looms in the mist obscure, and yet they know
It is not all illusion, for the dark
Sonorous sea sucks at the rocks below
And men grow deaf in age.

                    I'll not believe
That time can quench the ardour of the heart
Or bate one impulse out of youth, or grieve
Its mocked ideal dream. I will not part
With any sympathy for common things
That yesterday thought beautiful or good,
Not one enthusiasm that beauty brings
Will I let sleep, but die within this mood
Rather than lose another love I had,
Having so few surviving yesterday.

It is not all a dream. I will be glad
That there's some spirit treading upon earth
(Though scarcely heard, yet felt in every breath
Of the free air), a spirit of rebirth
In their own sons, for those who suffered death;
For there are poets wakening into song
And soldiers seeking peace on earth again,
I will believe in life while I am young,
For once grown old there's no believing then.

THE FRIEND

Because my deeper heart commands,
   To-night I leave this house of men
To find a brook to cleanse my hands
   And not to tread these streets again.

My old unhappy hope no more
   Shall search a passing stranger's eyes
To find the light it fainted for,
   But never see that light arise.

And now at last my lips shall end
   The long pretence of smile and speech,
For I will take that man for friend
   Whose love I need not to beseech.

We two will labour all day long,
   And sleep by night and rest at noon,
He will not mind my broken song
   When we tread homeward in the moon.

He will be pure in heart, and I
   Be strong in him, and in his trust
I shall not be a living lie :
   He will be just and I be just.

And though thereafter if the dream
   Hushed either heart within the breast,
Nor he nor I that hour would seem
   To grudge the other's greater rest.

A PROSPECT OF RETROSPECT

When I think how time will pass
Until this Now is turned to Then,
Like smoke that fades within a glass
Seem the curled fancies of my pen.

For this year's sturdy discontent
Will read in words a boy mis-spelled,
When I have weighed the Much life meant
Against the Little that it held.

SONNET

O Thou in the darkness far beyond the spheres
That seest me, puny, under the night below
Treading through Destiny to Death, forego
Thy triumph and glory for a score of years :
Leave me alive amid my hopes and fears,
The tempest of the mind, the joy, the woe,
That I may battle with myself and know
The worth of life, though be it by bitter tears.

Set not Thy stars against me whether I prove
Evil or good, ere from my inward spirit
Beauty and Truth depart, nor judge me less
In the full storm than in the calm thereof ;
Yet from the circle of earth that I inherit
O lift the shadow of this long loneliness !

SONNET

Now that the moonlight withers from the sky
Like hope within my heart, what's left to do
But dream alone until the day I die
On some imagined memory of you?
Believe there was a day when for a space
I looked into your unaverted eyes
To feel my spirit awake at their embrace
Articulate and beautiful and wise;
Or dream I hear your voice in the dim pause
Of dawn, ere birds awake, and feel your hand
Seek mine, when some night-fancy overawes
Your drowsy thoughts, knowing I understand :
Better to falsify you thus and rest
Than know myself forever dispossessed.

THE UNBORN SON

There is a tremor on the hills,
  The saplings stir within the wood,
The sunlight seeks the daffodils
  And I forget the things I rued.

Cheered by the promise of the spring
  I have foreseen my life's content,
Dreamed of a lovelier blossoming
  Than ever April gave to Lent.

In some far fairer spring than this
  Love will come home to me indeed;
My lips may waken in her kiss
  A flower from the sleeping seed.

And may be in some wintry night
  I shall wait helpless, no one by,
Nerved by anxiety's delight
  To hear amid the wind a cry . . .

A cry that snaps the thought of death
  And bursts the triple dark for me,
That with a glory in its breath
  Proclaims my immortality.

THE VIGIL

Beat on dull bell ! Mark me this feeble hour
   That cannot come again. Two . . . three . . .
     so soon !
And not an echo left to overpower
   The silence of a night without a moon.

By what last vanity of hope deceived
   Sought I to see her ? Now that earth's a dream
To mock the minds of men, who sleep aggrieved
   By their own crippled hearts, at what extreme

Of mad imagining love am I who sought
   Her house in this dark night ? There's not a
     sound
That whispers louder than my silent thought
   In all the world, even to the farthest bound.

How like a stone I stand, fixed, rigid, chill
   And yet not senseless, for I heard the chime—
When matters nothing, though I listen still :
   Maybe an hour's gone by . . . I'll count the
     time.

One minute . . . *two* . . . how dark the win-
    dows . . . *three* . . .
  Her house how dark . . . *four* now . . . perhaps
    she'll wake
And look across. But she'll not wake for thee
  Poor fool . . . *five*—let it go! . . . Not for thy
    sake . . .

Never, though Time on the meridian stops
  And thy long ranting's done; not waken then
Though such another darkness downward drops
  As this that hides her, never to rise again!

THE LETTERS

I have tied in the box with a rough twine of string
Her many letters to me, the hasty and gay
Scrawled in holiday mood, and the pensive lines
Drooping like threads for absence to hang upon,
Days and nights of slow irresolute hope,
So many beads flashing iridian light
On the neck of Time—these, and the scattering
    sparks
Dashed from the fire ere ever the wind had fallen
Or the river sobbed to sleep—I have shut them all
    in the box.

Her fancies shall people a world within it, and I
Some day, lifting the lid, shall suddenly see
The vague, familiar shadows stir in the light—
Cities and hills and fields with rivers between,
And flowers in the fields, and children playing
    around
With her sweet self in the midst. And whether
    I'll know

The name of anything then or recognise
The tallest figure of all to be myself,
Me, as her eyes once saw me, I dare not say.

Perhaps when I open the box they will fade away.

THE ENCHANTED HEART

Here blew winter once with the snowstorms
    spurning
Hill and furrow and field till all were whitened;
Here it was the robin flew away frightened
When I went by dreaming of spring returning.

Now that I walk on selfsame meadow and hill
Why seems winter the fairer, happier season,
And spring the very root of the mind's unreason?
Why do I ponder and roam unhappily still?

What do you lack to-day that you lacked not
    then,
O brooding heart, that you cannot be contented?
Far away, says the heart that was enchanted,
Long ago . . . in a dream . . . O never again!

JEFFERY DAY

Killed in Action 1918

" ON THE WINGS OF THE MORNING "

A sudden roar, a mighty rushing sound,
   a jolt or two, a smoothly sliding rise,
a tumbled blur of disappearing ground,
    and then all sense of motion slowly dies.
      Quiet and calm, the earth slips past below,
      as underneath a bridge still waters flow.

My turning wing inclines towards the ground;
   the ground itself glides up with graceful swing
and at the plane's far tip twirls slowly round,
    then drops from sight again beneath the wing
      to slip away serenely as before,
      a cubist-patterned carpet on the floor.

Hills gently sink and valleys gently fill.
   The flattened fields grow ludicrously small;
slowly they pass beneath and slower still
    until they hardly seem to move at all.
      Then suddenly they disappear from sight,
      hidden by fleeting wisps of faded white.

The wing-tips, faint and dripping, dimly show,
  blurred by the wreaths of mist that intervene.
Weird, half-seen shadows flicker to and fro
  across the pallid fog-bank's blinding screen.
    At last the choking mists release their hold,
    and all the world is silver, blue, and gold.

The air is clear, more clear than sparkling wine;
  compared with this wine is a turgid brew.
The far horizon makes a clean-cut line
  between the silver and the depthless blue.
    Out of the snow-white level reared on high
    glittering hills surge up to meet the sky.

Outside the wind-screen's shelter gales may race :
  but in the seat a cool and gentle breeze
blows steadily upon my grateful face,
  as I sit motionless and at my ease,
    contented just to loiter in the sun
    and gaze around me till the day is done.

And so I sit, half sleeping, half awake,
  dreaming a happy dream of golden days,
until at last, with a reluctant shake
  I rouse myself, and with a lingering gaze
    at all the splendour of the shining plain
    make ready to come down to earth again.

The engine stops : a pleasant silence reigns—
    silence, not broken, but intensified
by the soft, sleepy wires' insistent strains,
      that rise and fall, as with a sweeping glide
        I slither down the well-oiled sides of space,
        towards a lower, less enchanted place.

The clouds draw nearer, changing as they come.
    Now, like a flash, fog grips me by the throat.
Down goes the nose : at once the wires' low hum
      begins to rise in volume and in note,
        till, as I hurtle from the choking cloud
        it swells into a scream, high-pitched, and
            loud.

The scattered hues and shades of green and brown
    fashion themselves into the land I know,
turning and twisting, as I spiral down
      towards the landing ground ; till, skimming low,
        I glide with slackening speed across the
            ground,
        and come to rest with lightly grating sound.

GEOFFREY DEARMER

BIRDS

Eagles, you browless birds, who skim
The sky on poised and feathered limb,
You whom no sky's top terrifies,
Taught me the terror of the skies.

Cold cormorants, your spray-wet sheen,
Your cold bead eyes of glassy green,
And bubbling death-dive, swift and steep,
Taught me the terror of the deep.

Red-eyed, red-clawed, you vultures keen
Who find no carrion flesh unclean,
Who gather and cry at life's last breath,
Taught me the sanctity of death.

You whistling swans, your flapping flight,
A huge-formed arrow head of white
Over and down the horizon's dip,
Taught me the law of leadership.

You downy-eiders, from your breasts
Plucking the down to build your nests,
Taught me, as no commandment could,
The sacrifice of motherhood.

And you, live-crested cockatoos,
Grave toucans, hornbills and hoopoes;
Huge-billed, fixed-faced, preposterous birds,
Taught me God's wit, surpassing words.

UNSEEN

There was no sign, the landscape solid stood
And blown clouds frothed the sun's fall through
  a bath
Of claret merged with orange, yet the wood,
The stream, and every hillock, hedge, and path

I knew was full of life . . . an adder crept
And flickered like his own worm-flickering
  tongue;
The dewfall owl in darkening shadow slept;
Over the hill the swallow southward swung.

The boy-faced baby otters were at play;
The kingfisher had hidden his blaze of blue;
Hunching his back a weasel went his way;
I knew the wren was sleeping, and I knew

A bat unfurled his weft-winged sails and sped;
A harvest mouse swarmed up an ear of corn;
A snouted shrew-mouse in an owl's beak bled;
A bird was killed, another bird was born.

Without a sign or sound these things were done,
Beneath the sunset while I waited there;
But had I seen them starkly in the sun,
The sight could not have made me more aware.

JOHN DRINKWATER

SONNET

When all the hungry pain of love I bear,
And in poor lightless thought but burn and burn,
And wit goes hunting wisdom everywhere,
Yet can no word of revelation learn,
When endlessly the scales of yea and nay
In dreadful motion fall and rise and fall,
When all my heart in sorrow I could pay
Until at last were left no tear at all,
Then if with tame or subtle argument
Companions come and draw me to a place
Where words are but the tappings of content,
And life spreads all her garments with a grace,
I curse that ease, and hunger in my heart
Back to my pain and lonely to depart.

IN THE VALLEY

Let none devout forgive my sin
    Who have not sinned as I;
The soul immaculate within
    Has not to measure by
    My sorrowing husbandry.

The dark, the error, of my days
    Shall be consoled by none
That have not in forbidden ways
    Wandered as I have done
    With faces from the sun.

Princes of virtue, keep your skill
    Of pardon for your peers;
Frail with the frail I travel still
    Along uncertain years—
    Forbear your holy tears.

One hour in black Gethsemane
    I walked with Him alone.
He sees, He knows, He touches me—
    How shall it then be known
    To you, O hearts of stone?

WHO WERE BEFORE ME

Long time in some forgotten churchyard earth of
    Warwickshire,
My fathers in their generations lie beyond desire,
And nothing breaks the rest, I know, of John
    Drinkwater now,
Who left in sixteen-seventy his roan team at
    plough.

And James, son of John, is there, a mighty
    ploughman too,
Skilled he was at thatching and the barleycorn
    brew,
And he had a heart-load of sorrow in his day,
But ten score of years ago he put it away.

Then Thomas came, and played a fiddle cut of
    mellow wood,
And broke his heart, they say, for love that never
    came to good.

A hundred winter peals and more have rung
    above his bed—
O, poor eternal grief, so long, so lightly, com-
    forted.

And in the gentle yesterday these were but
    glimmering tombs,
Or tales to tell on fireside eves of legendary
    dooms;
I being life while they were none, what had their
    dust to bring
But cold intelligence of death upon my tides of
    Spring?

Now grief is in my shadow, and it seems well
    enough
To be there with my fathers, where neither fear
    nor love
Can touch me more, nor spite of men, nor my own
    teasing blame,
While the slow mosses weave an end of my for-
    forgotten name.

JOHN FREEMAN

THE EYE

It is not true that eyes
Save in the trembling eyelids' fall and rise
No meaning have. Did Eve
Hide in dull orbs the Snake's guile, and deceive
Adam with innocent stare?
When David saw how Bathsheba was fair
Burnt in his eyes no fire?
Marked not the men-at-arms his flushed desire
Sudden and swift upbrim,
That not the falling eyelids' cloud could dim?
And when Prince Absalon
Hung by those fatal locks, and help was none,
Under the nerveless lid
How could his father's agony be hid?
He heard the whisper, heard
The hushing, the renewed whisper, the one word :
And then was seen such gaze
As between madness and first wild grief sways,
Till " Absalon ! " and no sound
But " Absalon, my son, my son ! " crept róund.

167

It is not true that eyes
No meaning have but in the lids' fall and rise.
I have seen terror leap
Up from the spirit's unfathomable deep,
Through unfixed eyeballs stare,
Then shuddering sink back and lie snake-like
    there.
I have seen honour look
Swift under candid brows, when all else shook,
Pouring in warm light through
Eyes that from inward vision their seeing drew.
And I know the fluttering look
That first love flashes like a bird o'er a brook . . .
No lid so quick as to give
Speed to the glances that with lightning live.
And I know how the eyes,
Nameless, look on me out of clear dawn skies
And eve's unshadowy light—
Clear lidless eyes of pure immortal Sight,
Sweeping the million dew'd
Hill pastures and reluming the green-caved wood.

THE EVENING SKY IN MARCH

Rose-bosom'd and rose-limb'd,
With eyes of dazzling bright,
Shakes Venus 'mid the twined boughs of the
    night;
Rose-limb'd, soft stepping
From low bough to bough,
Shaking the wide-hung starry fruitage—dimmed
Its bloom of snow
By that sole planetary glow.

Venus, avers the astronomer
Not thus idly dancing goes
Flushing the eternal orchard with wild rose.
She through ether burns
Outpacing planetary earth,
And ere two years triumphantly returns
And again wave-like swelling flows;
And again her flashing apparition comes and goes.

This we have not seen,
No heavenly courses set,
No flight unpausing through a void serene :
But when eve clears,
Arises Venus as she first uprose
Stepping the shaken boughs among,
And in her bosom glows
The warm light hidden in sunny snows.

She shakes the clustered stars
Lightly, as she goes
Amid the unseen branches of the night,
Rose-limb'd, rose-bosom'd bright.
She leaps : they shake and pale; she glows—
And who but knows
How the rejoiced heart aches
When Venus all his starry wisdom shakes :

When through his mind
Tossing with random airs of an unearthly wind,
Rose-bosom'd, rose-limb'd,
The mistress of his starry vision arises,
And the boughs glittering sway
And the stars pale away,
And the enlarging heaven glows
As Venus light-foot 'mid the twined branches
    goes.

MOON BATHERS

Falls from her heaven the Moon, and stars sink
    burning
Into the sea where blackness rims the sea,
Silently quenched. Faint light that the waves
    hold
Is only light remaining; yet still gleam
The sands where those now-sleeping young moon-
    bathers
Came dripping out of the sea and from their arms
Shook flakes of light, dancing on the foamy edge
Of quiet waves. They were all things of light
Tossed from the sea to dance under the Moon—
Her nuns, dancing within her dying round,
Clear limbs and breasts silvered with Moon and
    waves
And quick with windlike mood and body's joy,
Withdrawn from alien vows, by wave and wind
Lightly absolved and lightly all forgetting.
    An hour ago they left. Remains the gleam
Of their late motion on the salt sea-meadow,
As loveliest hues linger when the sun's gone
And float in the heavens and die in reedy pools—
So slowly, who shall say when light is gone?

THE NIGHTINGALES

Musing upon imperishable things,
Honour and love and sorrow, as I walked
I came where water murmured of the hills
That flow down from the shoulders of the north
Into the shimmering green pool of the sea.
The unsteady water ran from the hill-shadows,
Itself a frightened shadow hurrying on
Into the starry clearness of May meads
All green and gold and sweet with opening buds.
The dew danced briefly between dusk and sun
But when the willow branches gave no shade
Save to the sleeping fins beneath the banks.
The rising wood waved " Come ! "

                      Then I passed in,
Plunging through sodden leaves and winter mire
That tardy May dried not, and leapt into
A sudden lake of blue—all sweet and heat
And wavering light—tall bluebells sunny-dappled
Whose pale green stems and folded buds and bells

Shaking out hue and odour drew the mind
Down into deep delights, to lie there swaying
Like amber weed fingered by every tide . . .
Faded those three grave visitants as I sank—
Honour and love and sorrow—and I watched
Their shadows slow withdrawing through a thin
Spinney beyond the shining lake. The boughs
Raking above netted the azure sky
And snared the clouds that turned and broke
        away
Torn by the branches or the fretting wind.
So cloud and leaf and air and light and bird
Flowed over me as I swayed sunken deep,
An idle weed fingered by every tide.

It was a nightingale above my head
Answering a nightingale unseen but near,
It was a nightingale that called me from
That sunken streaming of the sensual tide,
With notes like syllables in the silent mind
In silent night uttering things dear or sad.
But that unseen bird answered with the voice
Of smarting love, and crying, " Kiss me now
And bid all thoughts begone but thought of joys
Born of my lips ! " Yes, it was anxious love
Stealing the voice of that hid nightingale

And quickening sleepy memories with each note
Till the notes failed.

        Then the first singer poured
His song anew, pure, fresh, sustained—as though
Water-like it might fall all day, all night
Renewed, renewing. And I listening saw
Again those three shades from the spinney
    come—
Honour and love and sorrow—listening too
While that wild singer uttered yet his notes
So quick, and ranging wide 'tween earth and
    heaven,
That only thought could follow (even as shadow
Follows the flying feet of light from lake
To cool green hollow of the couched hills)—
Then paused, and called and ceased.

        How common seemed
That shining pool as I brushed by and shook
The shady dews from bended bells and snapped,
Heedless, the stems. The nightingale was gone,
And I pressed musing through the beamy wood,
And with me those three shadows whispering
One to another words that I could hear,
Half-understanding.

174

POSSESSION

I saw you,
I held you,
And surely I heard you :
But you were as far as any man living could be.

Though sometimes
I have seen you,
And touched you and heard you,
As together we walked and your sleeve now and
    then brushed mine;

Yet were you then
Farther, farther
Than with body's absence—
But who walks with you now while your thoughts
    are here and brush mine?

The slow waters
Of three oceans,
And the change of seasons,
Between us are but as a new-leafy hawthorn
    hedge,

And I see you
And hold you :—
But are you yet living,
Or come you now nearer than any man living
    may be?

NO MORE THAT ROAD

Now do I know
How newly-dead men go
As ragged ghosts among familiar ways,
Seeking to live again remembered days.

I see one stand,
Vale and Mount on either hand,
And saying, " Here I walked and walked with
    her;
Here was wheat, and hops here, and charlock
    there.

" Here was elder,
First-tinted berries of guelder.
Here, long before, wild apple flushed full pink.
Here broke that fire of violets, I think—

" Or was it—yes,
It was there they burned to death.
How all things burned that spring, and burned
    away,
As spring burned into summer, and then lay

" Glowing and prone,
With summer lovelier grown !
My heels with hers made rhyme upon the flint,
In music voice and silences were blent.

" And now, never,
Never, never, never, never,
Never again ! "   And turning away he aches,
And with old mortal sorrow his heart breaks;

Wishing he were
But one sad hour with her
On that salt road, and hill and vale and cloud,
Oast houses, orchards, violets, skylarks loud.

O, now I know
How one new-dead must go,
How in his haunted shadow-brain forever
Sounds the forsaken, " Never, never, never ! "

CATERPILLARS

Of caterpillars Fabre tells how day after day
Around the rim of a vast earth pot they crawled,
Tricked thither as they filed shuffling out one
    morn
Head to tail when the common hunger called.

Head to tail in a heaving ring day after day,
Night after slow night the starving mommets
    crept,
Each following each, head to tail day after day
An unbroken ring of hunger—then it was snapt.

I thought of you, long-heaving, horned green
    caterpillars,
As I lay awake. My thoughts crawled each after
    each,
Crawling at night each after each on the same
    nerve,
An unbroken ring of thoughts too sore for speech.

Over and over and over and over again
The same hungry thoughts and the hopeless same
    regrets,
Over and over the same truths, again and again
In a heaving ring returning the same regrets.

WILFRID WILSON GIBSON

BY THE WEIR

A scent of Esparto grass—and again I recall
The hour we spent by the weir of the paper-mill
Watching together the curving thunderous fall
Of frothing amber, bemused by the roar until
My mind was as blank as the speckless sheets that
    wound
On the hot steel ironing-rollers perpetually turn-
    ing
In the humming dark rooms of the mill : all sense
    and discerning
By the stunning and dazzling oblivion of hill-
    waters drowned.

And my heart was empty of memory and hope
    and desire
Till, rousing, I looked afresh on your face as you
    gazed—
Behind you an old gnarled fruit-tree in one still
    fire
Of innumerable flame in the sun of October
    blazed,

Scarlet and gold that the first white frost would
  spill
With eddying flicker and patter of dead leaves
  falling—
I looked on your face, as an outcast from Eden
  recalling
A vision of Eve as she dallied, bewildered and
  still,

By the serpent-encircled tree of knowledge that
  flamed
With gold and scarlet of good and evil, her eyes
Rapt on the river of life : then bright and un-
  tamed
By the labour and sorrow and fear of a world
  that dies
Your ignorant eyes looked up into mine, and I
  knew
That never our hearts should be one till your
  young lips had tasted
The core of the bitter-sweet fruit, and wise and
  toil-wasted
You should stand at my shoulder an outcast from
  Eden too.

WORLDS

Through the pale green forest of tall bracken-
    stalks,
Whose interwoven fronds, a jade-green sky,
Above me glimmer, infinitely high,
Towards my giant hand a beetle walks
In glistening emerald mail; and as I lie
Watching his progress through huge grassy blades
And over pebble boulders, my own world fades
And shrinks to the vision of a beetle's eye.

Within that forest world of twilight green
Ambushed with unknown perils, one endless day
I travel down the beetle-trail between
Huge glossy boles through green infinity . . .
Till flashes a glimpse of blue sea through the
    bracken asway,
And my world is again a tumult of windy sea.

FIRE

In each black tile a mimic fire's aglow,
And in the hearthlight old mahogany,
Ripe with stored sunshine that in Mexico
Poured like gold wine into the living tree
Summer on summer through a century,
Burns like a crater in the heart of night :
And all familiar things in the ingle-light
Glow with a secret strange intensity.

And I remember hidden fires that burst
Suddenly from the midnight while men slept,
Long-smouldering rages in the darkness nursed
That to an instant ravening fury leapt,
And the old terror menacing evermore
A crumbling world with fiery molten core.

LOUIS GOLDING

WHAT IS SO ODOROUS HERE?

What is so odorous here where I walk by?
Is it the tangle of firs at the edge of the soft
Smoothed meadow? Or the felled firs perhaps?
Or the abundance of flowers by the hollow bowery
    laps
Of the showery stream? Or an air from a piled
    hay-loft?
    None of these, none of these!
There were winds that blew from the farther
    wolds of the sky,
That had rustled the tops of tall imperious trees,
That had bent the heads of blue invisible flowers
Like faces bent for the kissing.
                  But none of these
Is odorous here as Love where I walk by.

A presence, a beauty, whom ear nor hand nor eye
   Gross with flesh can perceive—
You shall not know this thing that trembles by
   As more than an odour. Grieve,

Lumbering son of Eve,
For not the contours of peaks are so clear to the
    fleshless eye,
   Nor the song of larks so precise to the fleshless
       ear.
       Go by!
       Linger not here!

GERALD GOULD

If this were true, life's movement would rebel,
    And curdle to its source, as blood to the heart
    When the cold fires of indignation start
From their obscure lair in the body.—Well,
    If for us two to part were just to part,
All years would have one pointless tale to tell.

    *   *   *   *

I am frightened, sweetheart—that's the long and
        short
    Of the bad mind I bear : the scent comes back
    Of an unhappy garden gone to wrack,
The flower-beds trampled for an idiot's sport,
A mass of vermin batt'ning there, a mort
    Of weeds a-fester, all the green turned black,
    And through the sodden glades of loss and lack
The dead winds blown of hate and false report.

There was a music in the early air,
When our young love was virgin as we were,
    Ripe for the rose, new to the nightingale;
But now two ghosts walk showing each to each
The empty grace of ceremonious speech,
    And J am frightened, and the air is stale.

    *   *   *   *

If you were nothing but a sight to share,
   A coloured grace, a bird of beauty preening
   Pale flames of plumage in the overweening
Light of the insolent and crystal air,
Still to my thought you would be more than
     fair—
   But lo, compassionate, out of glory leaning,
   You have called forth the music and the
     meaning
From doubt, retreat, confusion and despair.

This is because you love me—all this scope
Of happy courage and insurgent hope,
   This simple power to understand and save,
This great contempt of shame, this careless trust
In the divine occasion of our dust—
   This is the strength that love to beauty gave.

     *   *   *   *

The silver mist along the river dims
   The middle landscape and the distant hills;
   It waxes imperceptibly, and fills
The evening with a sense of dreams and whims,
And great Orion of the starry limbs
   Is blotted out, and melancholy kills
   Earth's wandering hopes with its insistent
     chills,
And the late birds forget their twilight hymns.

The mist clings in your eyebrows and your hair—
    The silver starry web, the net of tears;
Your slim and startled body, unaware,
    Clings in my arms for warmth; a thousand
        fears
Torment the cloudy texture of the air,
    As, bit by bit, our known world disappears.

      *   *   *   *

I will believe the thing that you have said,
    Though chances challenge it and doubts deny,
    And every planet moving in the sky
Mock it with music; though my thoughts be led
Back and still back to that unhappy bed
    Where my first faith laid itself down to die;
    Though I be only such a thing as I,
And all the living laugh, and all the dead.

The ocean has its treasure, and the earth.
    I grudge to none his treasure—I have mine.
    In solitude and darkness I incline
To the last question of the final worth :
But stronger than all death of light is birth
    Of the one human light that burns divine.

      *   *   *   *

We shall live, maybe, till our world turns grey,
 And peace comes on us as our powers grow less,
 And scarce we shall distinguish happiness
From the opprobious process of decay :
Yet, 'mid the droop and pathos of that day,
 'Mid songs that cease and wings that acquiesce,
 The fading skies shall one last fire confess,
And love in a great sunset burn away.

Or else, perhaps, because we loved so well,
 And found love apt to life, the end will prove
  A consummation rather than a change;
And, tired in the twilight, we shall spell
 Familiar meanings from the text of love,
  And only find the words a little strange.

ROBERT GRAVES

THE ROCK BELOW

Comes a muttering from the earth
   Where speedwell grows and daisies grow,
" Pluck these weeds up, root and all,
   Search what hides below."

Root and all I pluck them out;
   There, close under, I have found
Stumps of thorn with ancient crooks
   Grappled in the ground.

I wrench the thorn-stocks from their hold
   To set a rose-bush in that place;
Love had pleasure in my roses
   For a summer space.

Yet the bush cries out in grief :
   " Our lowest rootlets turn on rock,
We live in terror of the drought
   Withering crown and stock."

I grow angry with my creature,
　Tear it out and see it die;
Far beneath I strike the stone,
　Jarring hatefully.

Impotently must I mourn
　Roses never to flower again?
Are heart and back too slightly built
　For a heaving strain?

Heave shall break my proud back never,
　Strain shall never burst my heart:
Steely fingers hook in the crack,
　Up the rock shall start.

Now from the deep and fruitful pit
Shoots forth the spring phoenix-tree
Long despaired in this bleak land,
Holds the air with boughs, with bland
　Fragrance welcome to the bee,
　With fruits of immortality.

A FORCED MUSIC

Of Love he sang, full-hearted one,
But when the song was done
The King demanded more,
Ay, and commanded more.
The boy found nothing for encore,
Words, melodies, none :
Ashamed the song's glad rise and plaintive fall
Had so charmed King and Queen and all.

He sang the same verse once again,
But urging less Love's pain,
With altered time and key
He showed variety,
Seemed to refresh the harmony
Of his only strain,
So still the glad rise and the plaintive fall
Could charm the King and Queen and all.

He of his song then wearying ceased,
But was not yet released ;

The Queen's request was *More*,
And her behest was *More*,
He played of random notes some score,
He found his rhymes at least—
Then suddenly let his twanging harp down fall
And fled in tears from King and Queen and all.

CHILDREN OF DARKNESS

(" In their generation wiser than the children
of Light.")

We spurred our parents to the kiss,
Though doubtfully they shrank from this—
Day had no courage to review
What lusty dark alone might do—
Then were we joined from their caress
In heat of midnight, one from two.

This night-seed knew no discontent,
In certitude his changings went;
Though there were veils about his face,
With forethought, even in that pent place,
Down towards the light his way he bent
To kingdoms of more ample space.

Was Day prime error, that regret
For darkness roars unstifled yet?
That in this freedom by faith won,
Only acts of doubt are done?
That unveiled eyes with tears are wet,
They loathe to gaze upon the sun?

A VILLAGE CONFLICT

The cottage damson laden as could be
Scowls at the Manor house magnolia tree
That year by year within its thoughtless powers
Yields flowers and leaves and flowers and leaves
    and flowers,
While the Magnolia shudders as in fear,
" *Figurez-vous!* two sackfuls every year! "

" THE GENERAL ELLIOTT "

He fell in victory's fierce pursuit,
   Holed through and through with shot,
A sabre sweep had hacked him deep
   'Twixt neck and shoulder-knot . . .

The potman cannot well recall,
   The ostler never knew,
Whether his day was Malplaquet,
   The Boyne, or Waterloo.

But there he hangs for tavern sign,
   With foolish bold regard
For cock and hen and loitering men
   And wagons down the yard.

Raised high above the hayseed world
   He smokes his painted pipe,
And now surveys the orchard ways,
   The damsons clustering ripe.

He sees the churchyard slabs beyond,
  Where country neighbours lie,
Their brief renown set lowly down;
  His name assaults the sky.

He grips the tankard of brown ale
  That spills a generous foam :
Oft-times he drinks, they say, and winks
  At drunk men lurching home.

No upstart hero may usurp
  That honoured swinging seat;
His seasons pass with pipe and glass
  Until the tale's complete.

And paint shall keep his buttons bright
  Though all the world's forgot
Whether he died for England's pride
  By battle, or by pot.

A LOVER SINCE CHILDHOOD

Tangled in thought am I,
Stumble in speech do I?
Do I blunder and blush for the reason why?
Wander aloof do I,
Lean over gates and sigh,
Making friends with the bee and the butterfly.

If thus and thus I do,
Dazed by the thought of you,
Walking my sorrowful way in the early dew,
My heart cut through and through
In this despair of you,
Starved for a word or a look will my hope renew,

Give then a thought for me
Walking so miserably,
Wanting relief in the friendship of flower or tree,
Do but remember, we
Once could in love agree,
Swallow your pride, let us be as we used to be.

THE PATCHWORK BONNET

Across the room my silent love I throw,
 Where you sit sewing in bed by candlelight,
  Your young stern profile and industrious
   fingers
Displayed against the blind in a shadow show,
 To Dinda's grave delight.

The needle dips and pokes, the cheerful thread
 Runs after, follow-my-leader down the seam :
  The patchwork pieces cry for joy together,
O soon to sit as a crown on Dinda's head,
 Fulfilment of their dream.

Snippets and odd ends folded by, forgotten,
 With camphor on a top shelf, hard to find,
  Now wake to this most happy resurrection,
To Dinda playing toss with a reel of cotton
 And staring at the blind.

Dinda in sing-song stretching out one hand
  Calls for the playthings; mother does not hear :
    Her minds sails far away on a patchwork
      Ocean,
And all the world must wait till she touches land,
  So Dinda cries in fear.

Then Mother turns, laughing like a young fairy,
  And Dinda smiles to see her look so kind,
    Calls out again for playthings, playthings,
      playthings,
And now the shadows make an Umbrian " *Mary
Adoring*," on the blind.

THE TREASURE BOX

Ann in chill moonlight unlocks
Her polished brassbound treasure-box,
Draws a soft breath, prepares to spread
The toys around her on the bed.
She dips for luck : by luck pulls out
A silver pig with ring in snout,
The sort that Christmas puddings yield;
Next comes a painted nursery shield
Boy-carved; and then two yellow gloves,
A Limerick wonder that Ann loves,
Leather so thin and joined so well
The pair fold in a walnut shell;
Here's patchwork that her sister made
With antique silk and flower brocade,
Small faded scraps in memory rich
Joined each to each with feather-stitch;
Here's cherry and forget-me-not
Ribbon bunched in a great knot;
A satin purse with pansies on it;
A Tudor baby's christening bonnet;
Old Mechlin lace minutely knit
(Some woman's eyes went blind for it);

And Spanish broideries that pinch
Three blossomed rose-trees to one inch;
Here are Ann's brooches, simple pins,
A Comet brooch, two Harlequins,
A Posy; here's a great resplendent
Dove-in-bush Italian pendant;
A Chelsea gift-bird; a toy whistle;
A halfpenny stamped with the Scots thistle;
A Breguet watch; a coral string;
Her mother's thin-worn wedding ring;
A straw box full of hard smooth sweets;
A book, the *Poems of John Keats*;
A chessman; a pink paper rose;
A diary dwindling to its close
Nine months ago; a worsted ball;
A patchbox; a stray match—that's all,
All but a few small treasured scraps
Of paper; things forbid perhaps—
See how slowly Ann unties
The packet where her heartache lies;
Watch her lips move; she slants a letter
Up towards the moon to read it better,
(The moon may master what he can).
R stands for Richard, A for Ann,
And L . . . at this the old moon blinks
And softly from the window shrinks.

IVOR GURNEY

THOUGHTS OF NEW ENGLAND

Gloucester streets walking in Autumn twilight,
Past Kineburgh's cottage and old Raven Tavern,
That Hoare he kept, the Puritan, who tired
Or fired, and took a passage in the " Mayflower,"
Gloucester streets walking in frost-clear hour—
Of " Captains Courageous " as a boy read, think-
    ing,
And sea-ports, ships, and all that boy desired . . .
Walt Whitman, history-scraps and Huck Finn's
    cavern :
My thought went wandering how the New Eng-
    land Folk
Walked twilight now, watched stars steady or
    blinking—
If thoughts came Eastward as mine Westward
    went.
Of our " Citizen," the " Massachusetts Times,"
And the boys crying them perhaps about their
    lanes.
But those no historied ground of Roman or
    Danes.

What are the streets that have no memories,
That are not underset by ancient rubbish?
Where gables overhang, and the quarters clang
From Cathedral towers, and the slops or dinner
    dish,
Hurried a man voids handily into the gutter:
And ghosts haunt the streets and of old troubles
    mutter.
Where steel and scarlet of the military
And routine use flash vivid momentarily;
Imagination stricken unaccountably
At full day into pictures not looked for even,
And children from their play by curfew driven.

Are there men of my blood over Atlantic
Wondering there what light is growing thick
By Severn and what real thing Cotswold is?
Are there men walking slow till tiredness leads
    in
To write or read till the night's veil grows
    thin;
Insatiate desiring what hope would win?
Is the air clear there as Thoreau's prose,
With frost and sparkling water, and day's close
As mild, as soft as shows in " Evangeline "?
(Since all verse from the air or earth does win).

Do they hear tell of Domesday Book, and not
Think of this Gloucester where the scrivener
    wrote
Command of reeves first set their lists to begin?
Do they wish walk at evening where the earls
    went in
And William : Are there not crowns of England
    old
That first in Gloucester's Abbey showed their
    gold?
Can villas contain men in unloving hold
As here the cornered, the nooked low-ceilinged
    beetle-browed
Houses cloak man in; or the strict thoroughfares
Stone or asphalt paved ally to man?

Are there great joys in April her high days
For those who cannot high imaginations see
Of other men builded, stirred to a great praise?
Cotswold earthing profound for white material,
Masses of stone gone slender as a silver birch,
Upwards in dazzle to an arching azure.

O where in the new town shall recompense come,
For the market-days, the week-end trouble with-
    out measure,

The crowded four ways and cattle markets boom.
And country faces seen often with so much
pleasure ?

Can New England think deep thoughts of her
bye-ways,
Is Abana and Pharpar a balance for
Severn receiving Avon, at her knot of highways,
Her Abbey township, beneath so high a cloud
floor ?

But nevertheless one would go very willingly
At the year's turn, where Washington or Lincoln
walked,
Or praise " Drum Taps " or " This Compost,"
and hear talked
Speech of Lowell, or Hawthorne, or Holmes and
be
Pleased with citizenship of Gloucester or Wor-
cester
And companionship of veterans or veterans' sons
Of the Wilderness or Richmond, see the old guns
That set Chattanooga's thronged woods astir ;
Or woke terror in steadfastness with red anger.

But not for longer than the strangeness lasted.
Severn yet calls not to be resisted :
And the mix of Dane thoughts, Roman, with
    Middle-Age
Calls all love out to mark on any page
The glory of Peter's Abbey high up in Summer,
Or low in Winter's gloom, and a wavering shape,
Are more than is ever seen for foreign comer
To Connecticut, or Staten or Providence with its
    cape,
Being loveliness and history and height in one.

And there is nothing uprooted that is not
    changed.
Better to stay and wonder in the half light
How New England saunters where Kipling loved
    and ranged,
And watch the starling flocks in first autumn
    flight.

The New World has qualities its own,
But the Old not yet decrepit or withered is
    grown,
And brick and timber of age five centuries known
Are consolation for poverty enough

Against New York, where they say Opera is
    brilliant,
And the byeways with five dollar notes are
    strown.
The stuff of Liberty is a varying stuff,
But from Grant's men, Lee's men, noblemen
    should never want.

SMUDGY DAWN

Smudgy dawn scarfed with military colours
Northward, and flowing wider like slow sea
    water,
Woke in lilac and elm and almost among garden
    flowers.
Birds a multitude; increasing as it made lighter.
Nothing but I moved by railings there; slept
    sweeter
Than kings the country folk in thatch or slate
    shade,
Peace had the grey West, fleece clouds sure in its
    power,
Out on much-Severn I thought waves readied for
    laughter
And the fire-swinger promised behind elm pillars
A day worthy such beginning to come after.

DAWN

Dawn came not surprising, but later widened
To great space and a sea of many colours
With slate and pink and blue above the
    frightened
Mud fields soiled and heavy with War's colours—
And the guns thumped and threatened,
While the bacon frizzled, and the warm incense
    heightened,
Drifting in bays and dugouts slowly lightened.
First light bringing the thought what familiar
    star
There was, of town, farm, cottage, over there,
    over yonder,
And by day before duty settled awhile to
A companionship of good talk, forgetting night's
    woe.

GEORGE ROSTREVOR HAMILTON

FOG

Ten paces round me solid earth stretches,
 Moving as I move through impalpable regions
Of space unbounded, unreal, untenanted,
Or tenanted, if tenanted, by powerless anatomies,
 Unbreathing hosts, phantom legions.

Ochreous lights hang, stars of an underworld,
 In the bronze vapour. Unsupported branches
Trail a thin tapestry. Softly, a footfall !
Passes a shadow, a tall shadow—what memory,
 As of a fierce dream, her face blanches?

So to Æneas, moving obscurely
 Through the dim groves and Avernian
   meadows,
So may have shone the white face of Dido,
Silently scorning him, scorning his entreaties—
 Then fled away through crowding shadows.

ENVIRONMENT

The faint clouds overrun with gold
More copious than they can hold;
The river, gathering deeper light,
Smoulders upon the verge of night.
The darkening elm trees by the bank
Stand in a hushed and solemn rank,
But in this world of other worlds' tones,
Men loll at ease and boys throw stones.

MULTIPLICITY

When I invade my secret soul
Thinking to find it clean and whole,
There peep at me from cave and den
So many phantoms of half-men
That I, lest those companions gaunt
My laughing work-a-day self should haunt,
Rush out again to the world, to see
A saner multiplicity.

THE CANDLE

When at a glance my body's eye
Runs from East to West the sky
And gathers in one swift embrace
A million shining miles of space,
Then I do wonder that my mind,
Straining her eyes before, behind—
A trembling candle—should illume
So dusty and so small a room.

FRANK KENDON

NOW TO THE WORLD

Now to the world we'll go, my body and I,
Leaving the comfortable nights and days,
The books where wise old men in wise old ways
Wrote down their thoughts of life in years gone
    by.

Snap up the switch, and let the darkness down;
Shut the two doors; deliver up the key.
These things pass on to others; but for me
They have grown lifeless—I must seek my own.

Picture and book, most taciturn, most dear;
Hearth where I burned my more ambitious
    rhymes;
Room where I dreamed of life a thousand times;
Scene of so many a joy and fancied fear,

There is no break in this farewell. I go,
Eager as sailors to the uncharted sea—
To wreck or Eldorado—steadfastly;
Whither, save hence, I do not care nor know.

Here I have laid my little-practised hand
To many a task, as children play, for learning;
Here I have told my closest secrets, burning
With strong affection for some intimate friend.

Here we have laughed, or argued, man with man,
Till the quick double pulse of midnight sounded;
Have mocked at Time and Death, and been
        confounded;
Have spoken glibly of the race we ran.

And here, in silence, as the impatient morning
Hovered behind the elms, I spoke with Sorrow;
Clung to wild prophecies of hope to-morrow;
Prayed to I know not Whom, and met day
        scorning.

Here it was hard to lose, if only dreams;
And here, where empty walls return my stare,
A strong imagination, passionate, clear,
Opened a window upon love, it seems:

Better than art, by trembling fingers made,
The portrait of a queen without her crown,
A thing alive, with magic looks cast down,
And moving lips, by cunning truth portrayed . . .

Close the two doors. Deliver up the key.
There is no break in this farewell to peace—
No frown or smile to signify release—
Snap up the switch; and let the darkness see!

THE BACKWATER

Though quietness, though quietness of mien
Lay like a mask upon my features, brother,
And though the idle, random, easy words
Fell from our lips, like water dropping slowly
Over the fern leaves on some forest pond—
You read my secret falsely. True, the place
Was peace imbued; the hour, the time of year,
The smoothed-out leisure, the enormous dreams
Of trees upon the undulating water,
The " vorld-without-end " cooing of the doves
Hidden in summer's highth (the Milton word
That sounded smoothly of sweet antiquity)—
All these were symbols, fencing in our thoughts
To short tranquility. The scarcely swaying punt
Hung between verdant roof and dark reflection;
Up or down, the everlasting heavens
Peered between vaulted boughs upon us there.
If there is cool content on this round earth
Here must her harbour be : here might she come
To refuge from the fierce pulsation of
The noonday meadows, or the noisy streets;

And like Ophelia, garlanded with flowers,
Float crooning on the stream. And here lay we
Unconscious of the world and its long questions,
Unconscious of the steady lapse of summer,
Unconscious of our breathing even; of life
Thinking no bitterness; and dead to death.

   The beauty of the river taunted me,
Struck low, preluding chords upon my sense,
And left the theme unfinished. It was madness
Fathoming beauty's purpose; maddening
With our poor human gifts to try to close
A fugue so finely started; maddening
To read the full solemnity of peace
On trees above, to watch content below
Come stealing by on breathing waves, on winds
To feel content waft down, to fill our eyes
With colours of content, and yet, alas !
Never in either human heart to know
The friendly whisper of the wished-for guest.

I do not know what restless questioning
Ran through your mind in that uneasy ease,
Only you seemed no happier than you dared,
As though the very trees might enviously
Come crashing down if you should quite usurp
Their sole prerogative, and be content.

Nor you, my foster-brother, guessed what lay
Hidden behind my summer languid eyes;
But seemed at times to envy me my mood.

O there's a gulf abysmal, dark and wide,
Forever fixed between the oldest friends,
And the impossible a soul longs after
Is to build bridges there, where none may
    build.
I almost hated beauty, I so loved her;
Night and day courted her, paid secret service
Year upon year before her haunting face,
Thinking no evil of so wonderful
A creature. Here in this quiet place
She stooped and mocked, and grew more fair in
    mocking.
Knew she what men may never know of us :
The hunger and the endless disappointment,
Desire and its eternal unfulfilment,
Fidelity to hopes that reason sneers at,
This loneliness? While you, whom I have
    known
And shared some hopes with, reading all about
In air and fretted sky and foliage,
And in the placid river, deep content—
You, with a heart so haunted, read in me

The symbolism of the summer time
That breathed about us; envied me indeed
A quiet that both lacked, that both desired
The unwilling hour to teach us, but in vain.

THE IMMIGRANT

When Ruth was old
She'd take her children's children on her knee.
They never wearied to be told
Tales of her girlhood in a far country.

For though her eyes grew dim
Men said of her : " Her heart is always young."
And Boaz, while she spoke to him,
Loved the faint accent of a foreign tongue.

THE KERNEL

Now that the flush of summer is gone,
And in the lane no flower is seen,
  No hedge in leaf ,
No tree in gold or green;

Now that the golden fruit is stored,
And in the wood no song is heard,
  No merry stir
Of song from any bird;

Now that the uncompanioned wind
Blows cold across the naked land,
  And, hung in black,
Bare trees like mourners stand;

Winter reveals through falling rain,
A strength which summer had left unseen :
  Beauty and peace
Which, but for tears, had been in vain,
Which, but for loss, had never been.

SONNET

Now splendidly the earth awakes to vigour,
Music and scent and colour flood the land,
And fields of naked soil no more disfigure
The skylark's sunlit prospects. Buds are fanned
Into a timid verdure, and a haze
Of delicate green imbues the far-away woods;
The cuckoo has begun to count his days,
The wind-flowers dance by the pale arum hoods
Swiftly the sombre winter landscape alters,
More gradual change, and lovelier far than dawn ;
Nothing departs, or fades, and nothing falters,
Only the cold despair of death is flown.
  Courage, impatient heart; in thy despair
  There shall be wrought a miracle as fair.

SONNET

Weary of play, some summer eve, may chance
You will come running in from dewless lawns,
The long day's laughter in your countenance;
(O laughing eyes, where brighter beauty dawns !)
And taking up this book, as one might take
A leaf or flower or blade of grass while speaking,
Read lightly on, a word or two, and make
No meaning of them; little meaning seeking.
There standing, bending head and straying hair,
As leaf by leaf you idly turn these over,
Love, love—the word will meet you everywhere,
And you will laugh, remembering your lover;
And take the book, perhaps, being tired of play,
To wonder and read till daylight dies away.

PALESTINE

Oh, we speak not overmuch
Of the strange lands we have seen,
Our eyes were not for such
    Very keen.

And the brightest thing we knew,
In a land of gaudy flowers,
Was a daisy, tipped with dew,
    English! Ours!

THE EXCUSE

Beauty of form, of lip, of cheek, of eye, of word,
    of deed,
Not for thou hast, though thou hast these, I love
    thee—this were choice;
Thou art my mistress for no cause : I love because
    I need;
But praise, to still my questing mind, thy looks,
    thy grace, thy voice.

THE ORANGE

Take him this charm.
Though he sits long and languidly to-night,
Wrapped in Lethean thoughtlessness,
He will awake; his eyes will twinkle; bright
    Will glow his cheeks; and, warm
His lively blood will dance away distress.

    Then you shall hear
Of violet, vaulted skies, and brazen days;
And catch the whisper in the shadowy groves
Of warmly scented wind that lightly plays
    Among the oranges and near
The lapping waves of Yafa this man loves.

    Then you shall see
The pale rose mosque, the white-walled dusty
        street,
Swart copper skin, and gleaming stalwart arm,
Bright-turbaned babes, and laughing teeth, and
        sweet
    Rachels whose modesty
Droops over tremulous eyes. . . . Take him this
        charm.

I SPEND MY DAYS VAINLY

I spend my days vainly,
 Not in delight;
Though the world is elate,
 And tastes her joys finely.

Here wrapped in slow musing
 Lies my dark mind,
To no music attuned
 Save its own, and despising

The lark for remoteness,
 The thrush for bold lying,
The soft wind for blowing,
 And the round sun for brightness.

O tarry for me, sweet;
 I shall stir, I shall wake!
And the melody you seek
 Shall be lovely, though late.

WILLIAM KERR

COUNTING SHEEP

Half-awake I walked
A dimly-seen sweet hawthorn lane
Until sleep came;
I lingered at a gate and talked
A little with a lonely lamb.
He told me of the great still night,
Of calm starlight,
And of the lady moon, who'd stoop
For a kiss sometimes;
Of grass as soft as sleep, of rhymes
The tired flowers sang:
The ageless April tales
Of how, when sheep grew old,
As their faith told,
They went without a pang
To far green fields, where fall
Perpetual streams that call
To deathless nightingales.
  And then I saw, hard by,
A shepherd lad with shining eyes,
And round him, gathered one by one

Countless sheep, snow-white;
More and more they crowded
With tender cries,
Till all the field was full
Of voices and of coming sheep.
Countless they came, and I
Watched, until deep
As dream-fields lie
I was asleep.

THE AUDIT

Mere living wears the most of life away :
Even the lilies take thought for many things,
For frost in April and for drought in May,
And from no careless heart the skylark sings.

Those cheap utilities of rain and sun
Describe the foolish circle of our years,
Until death takes us, doing all undone,
And there's an end at last to hopes and fears.

Though song be hollow and no dreams come true,
Still songs and dreams are better than the truth :
But there's so much to get, so much to do,
Mary must drudge like Martha, dainty Ruth

Forget the morning music in the corn,
And Rachel grudge when Leah's boys are born.

D. H. LAWRENCE

KANGAROO

In the northern hemisphere
Life seems to leap at the air, or skim under the
    wind
Like stags on rocky ground, or pawing horses, or
    spring scut-tailed rabbits.

Or else rush horizontal to charge at the sky's
    horizon,
Like bulls or bisons or wild pigs.

Or slip like water slippery towards its ends,
As foxes, stoats, and wolves, and prairie dogs.

Only mice, and moles, and rats, and badgers, and
    beavers, and perhaps bears
Seem belly-plumbed to the earth's mid-navel.
Or frogs that when they leap come flop, and flop
    to the centre of the earth.

But the yellow antipodal Kangaroo, when she sits
    up,
Who can unseat her, like a liquid drop that is
    heavy, and just touches earth.

The downward drip.
The down-urge.
So much denser than cold-blooded frogs.

Delicate mother Kangaroo
Sitting up there rabbit-wise, but huge, plumb-
      weighted,
And lifting her beautiful slender face, oh! so
      much more gently and finely lined than a
      rabbit's, or than a hare's,
Lifting her face to nibble at a round white
      peppermint drop, which she loves, sensitive
      mother Kangaroo.

Her full antipodal eyes, so dark,
Her sensitive, long, pure-bred face.
So big and quiet and remote, having watched so
      many empty dawns in silent Australia.

Her little loose hands, and drooping Victorian
      shoulders.
And then her great weight below the waist, her
      vast pale belly
With a thin young yellow little paw hanging out,
      and straggle of a thin long ear, like ribbon,

Like a funny trimming to the middle of her belly,
   thin little dangle of an immature paw, and
   one thin ear.
Her belly, her big haunches
And in addition the great muscular python
   stretch of her tail.

There, she shan't have any more peppermint
   drops.
So she wistfully, sensitively sniffs the air, and
   then turns and goes off in slow sad leaps

On the long flat skis of her legs,
Steered and propelled by that steel-strong snake
   of a tail.

Stops again, half turns, inquisitive to look back.
While something stirs quickly in her belly, and a
   lean little face comes out, as from a window,
Peaked, and a bit dismayed,
Only to disappear again quickly away from the
   sight of the world, to snuggle down in the
   warmth,
Leaving the trail of a different paw hanging out.

Still she watches with eternal, cocked wistfulness !

How full her eyes are, like the full, fathomless,
   shining eyes of an Australian black-boy
Who has been lost so many centuries on the
   margins of existence !

She watches with insatiable wistfulness.
Untold centuries of watching for something to
   come,
For a new signal from life, in that silent lost land
   of the South.

Where nothing bites but insects and snakes and
   the sun, small life.
Where no bull roared, no cow ever lowed, no stag
   cried, no leopard screeched, no lion coughed,
   no dog barked,
But all was silent except for parrots occasionally,
   in the haunted blue bush.

Wistfully watching, with wonderful liquid eyes.
And all her weight, all her blood, dripping sack-
   wise down towards the earth's centre,
And the live little one taking in its paw at the
   door of her belly.

Leap then, and come down on the line that draws
   to the earth's deep, heavy centre.

D. H. LAWRENCE

SNAKE

A snake came to my water trough
On a hot, hot day, and I in pyjamas for the heat,
To drink there.

In the deep, strange-scented shade of the great
    dark carob-tree
I came down the steps with my pitcher
And must wait, must stand and wait, for there
    he was at the trough before me.

He reached down from a fissure in the earth-wall
    in the gloom
And trailed his yellow-brown slackness soft-
    bellied down, over the edge of the stone
    trough
And rested his throat upon the stone bottom,
And where the water had dripped from the tap,
    in a small clearness,
He sipped with his straight mouth,

259

Softly drank through his straight gums, into his
    slack long body,
Silently.

Someone was before me at my water trough,
And I, like a second comer, waiting.

He lifted his head from his drinking, as cattle do,
And looked at me vaguely, as drinking cattle do,
And flickered his two-forked tongue from his lips,
    and mused a moment,
And stooped and drank a little more,
Being earth brown, earth golden from the burn-
    ing burning bowels of the earth
On the day of Sicilian July, with Etna smoking.

The voice of my education said to me
He must be killed,
For in Sicily the black, black snakes are innocent,
    the gold are venomous.

And voices in me said, If you were a man
You would take a stick and break him now, and
    finish him off.

But I must confess how I liked him,
How glad I was he had come like a guest in quiet,
      to drink at my water-trough
And depart peaceful, pacified, and thankless,
Into the burning bowels of this earth?

Was it cowardice, that I dared not kill him?
Was it perversity, that I longed to talk to him?
Was it humility, to feel so honoured?
I felt so honoured.

And yet those voices:
If you were not afraid, you would kill him!

And truly I was afraid, I was most afraid,
But even so, honoured still more
That he should seek my hospitality
From out the dark door of the secret earth.

He drank enough
And lifted his head, dreamily, as one who has
      drunken,
And flickered his tongue like a forked night on the
      air, so black,
Seeming to lick his lips,
And looked around like a god, unseeing, into the
      air,

And slowly turned his head,
And slowly, very slowly, as if thrice adream,
Proceeded to draw his slow length curving round
And climb again the broken bank of my wall-face.

And as he put his head into that dreadful hole,
And as he slowly drew up, snake-easing his
    shoulders, and entered farther,
A sort of horror, a sort of protest against his
    withdrawing into that horrid black hole,
Deliberately going into the blackness, and slowly
    drawing himself after,
Overcame me now his back was turned.

I looked round, I put down my pitcher,
I picked up a clumsy log
And threw it at the water-trough with a clatter.

I think it did not hit him,
But suddenly that part of him that was left
    behind convulsed in undignified haste,
Writhed like lightning, and was gone
Into the black hole, the earth-lipped fissure in
    the wall-front,
At which, in the intense still noon, I stared with
    fascination.

And immediately I regretted it.
I thought how paltry, how vulgar, what a mean
  act !
I despised myself and the voices of my accursed
  human education.

And I thought of the albatross,
And I wished he would come back, my snake.

For he seemed to me again like a king,
Like a king in exile, uncrowned in the under-
  world,
Now due to be crowned again.

And so, I missed my chance with one of the lords
Of life.
And I have something to expiate;
A pettiness.

MAN AND BAT

When I went into my room, at mid-morning,
Say ten o'clock . . .
My room, a crash-box over that great stone rattle
The Via de' Bardi . . .

When I went into my room at mid-morning
Why? . . . a bird!

A bird
Flying round the room in insane circles.

In insane circles !
. . . A bat!

A disgusting bat
At mid-morning ! . . .

Out! Go out!

264

Round and round and round
With a twitchy, nervous, intolerable flight,
And a neurasthenic lunge,
And an impure frenzy;
A bat, big as a swallow.

Out, out of my room!

The venetian shutters I push wide
To the free, calm upper air;
Loop back the curtains . . .

Now, out, out from my room!

So to drive him out, flicking with my white
     handkerchief: *Go!*
But he will not.

Round and round and round
In an impure haste,
Fumbling, a beast in air,
And stumbling, lunging and touching the walls,
   the bell-wires
About my room!

Always refusing to go out into the air
Above that crash-gulf of the Via de' Bardi,
Yet blind with frenzy, with cluttered fear.

At last he swerved into the window bay,
But blew back, as if an incoming wind blew him
    in again.
A strong inrushing wind.

And round and round and round!
Blundering more insane, and leaping, in throbs,
    to clutch at a corner,
At a wire, at a bell-rope:
On and on, watched relentless by me, round and
    round in my room,
Round and round and dithering with tiredness
    and haste and increasing delirium
Flicker-splashing round my room.

I would not let him rest;
Not one instant cleave, cling like a blot with his
    breast to the wall
In an obscure corner,
Not an instant!

I flicked him on,
Trying to drive him through the window.

Again he swerved into the window bay
And I ran forward to frighten him forth.
But he rose, and from a terror worse than me he
　　flew past me
Back into my room, and round, round, round in
　　my room
Clutch, cleave, stagger,
Dropping about the air
Getting tired.

Something seemed to blow him back from the
　　window
Every time he swerved at it;
Back on a strange parabola, then round, round,
　　dizzy in my room.

He *could* not go out,
I also realised . . .
It was the light of day which he could not enter.
Any more than I could enter the white-hot door
　　of a blast-furnace.

He could not plunge into the daylight that
　　streamed at the window.
It was asking too much of his nature.

Worse even than the hideous terror of me with
    my handkerchief,
Saying : *Out, go out!*
Was the horror of white daylight in the window !

So I switched on the electric light, thinking : *Now*
The outside will seem brown . . .

But no.
The outside did not seem brown.
And he did not mind the yellow electric light.

Silent!
He was having a silent rest.
But never!
Not in my room.

Round and round and round
Near the ceiling as if in a web,
Staggering;
Plunging, falling out of the web,
Broken in heaviness,
Lunging blindly,
Heavier;
And clutching, clutching for one second's pause,
Always, as if for one drop of rest,
One little drop.

And I !
Never, I say . . .
Go out!

Flying slower,
Seeming to stumble, to fall in air.
Blind-weary.

Yet never able to pass the whiteness of light into
    freedom . . .
A bird would have dashed through, come what
    might.

Full, sink, lurch, and round and round
Flicker, flicker-heavy;
Even wings heavy :
And cleave in a high corner for a second, like a
    clot, also a prayer.

But no
Out, you beast.

Till he fell in a corner, palpitating, spent.
And there, a clot, he squatted and looked at me.
With sticking-out, bead-berry eyes, black,
And improper derisive ears,
And shut wings,
And brown, furry body.

Brown, nut-brown, fine fur!
But it might as well have been a hair on a spider; thing
With long, black-paper ears.

So, a dilemma!
He squatted there like something unclean.

No, he must not squat, nor hang, obscene, in my room!

Yet nothing on earth will give him courage to pass the sweet fire of day.

What then?
Hit him and kill him and throw him away?

Nay,
I didn't create him.
Let the God that created him be responsible for his death . . .
Only, in the bright day, I will not have this clot in my room.

Let the God who is maker of bats watch with them in their unclean corners . . .
I admit a God in every crevice,
But not bats in my room;
Nor the God of bats, while the sun shines.

So out, out you brute! . . .
And he lunged, flight-heavy, away from me,
   sideways, *a sghembo!*
And round and round and round my room, a clot
   with wings,
Impure even in weariness.

Wings dark skinny and flapping the air,
Lost their flicker.
Spent.

He fell again with a little thud
Near the curtain on the floor.
And there lay.

Ah death, death
You are no solution!
Bats must be bats.

Only life has a way out.
And the human soul is fated to wide-eyed
   responsibility
In life.

So I picked him up in a flannel jacket,
Well covered, lest he should bite me.

For I would have had to kill him if he'd bitten
    me, the impure one . . .
And he hardly stirred in my hand, muffled up.

Hastily, I shook him out of the window.

And away he went!
Fear craven in his tail.
Great haste, and straight, almost bird straight
    above the Via de' Bardi.
Above that crash-gulf of exploding whips,
Towards the Borgo San Jacopo.

And now, at evening, as he flickers over the river,
Dipping with petty triumphant flight, and titter-
    ing over the sun's departure,
I believe he chirps, pipistrello, seeing me here on
    this terrace writing :
There he sits, the long loud one!
But I am greater than he . . .
I escaped him . . .

E. R. R. LINKLATER

THE FAITHLESS SHEPHERD

With nice observance of the rules
And precepts of the pastoral schools,
A shepherdess, as fair as pure,
Beneath a hedgerow sat demure.
With conscious grace before her feet
Her swain lay faithfully supine,
Essaying neatly to combine
Positions patently discreet
With rustic notions of design.

Hedge-high the wild small roses grew
To kiss the breeze, and yet there blew
In Phœbe's cheek a wilder rose
That Corin watered with his woes.

Of sighs and chosen words he twined
A cunning thread to trap and bind
The bird that sang in Phœbe's heart;
With careful hand he spread the lime,
The tuneful tears, the weary rhyme,

Of tattered, patched Italian art,
And tirelessly reset the snare
Of piping music's gusty ware.

Yet loving he observed the rules
Laid down for use in pastoral schools,
And all advantages eschewed
        Of Phœbe's solitude.

And still in spite of poetry
And this too subtle courtesy,
She tarried coldly continent;
No signal of surrender flamed,
Though orthodoxy clearly claimed
        A maidenly consent.

There stood in shade of friendly grass
A jug with sweet cool wine a-brim,
And, weary of his Lover's Mass,
Tall Corin took the sacrament
A readier chalice offered him.
The honest wine first cooled his head,
And led back laughter that had fled
The solemn ritual of love.

And in a little while
The countryside, that once had been
A placidly enamelled screen,
He saw as mile on waving mile
Of grass that grew more richly green,
Of flowers and jolly rotund hills,
Of deeply chuckling meadow-rills,
And marching roads; while far above
The portly clouds that statelily
Had stalked across the level sky,
Were tripped and tumbled by the wind
    In coltish merriment.

Till, peering through the wine, half-blind
And swimming up in slow ascent,
The bottom of the honest jug
Appears like Truth, all soft and snug
And pinkly naked in her well.

Then Corin laughs. His glances dwell
Once more on Phœbe, and he sees
The wild-rose flaming in her cheek.
And now no more on pilgrim knees
He pleads a docile love and meek,
But boldly clips her in his arms
And quiets her modest faint alarms

With kiss on eager kiss that sips
The rose-red nectar of her lips.
And now his love grows kind to feel
The soft white arms that slowly steal
About his neck. Now Phœbe's kisses,
Each one Love's virgin young Ulysses,
In turn seek rest on Corin's lips . . .

A vagrant cloud for mockery
Slid solemnly athwart the sun,
And in the leaves, half-breathlessly,
A tiny breeze hid shivering.
Hedge-high the small wild roses flare,
Whose petals, gravely curtseying,
Blow softly down on Phœbe's hair . . .

And still the bottom of the jug,
With innocent unwinking eye,
Stared nakedly into the sky.

SYLVIA LYND

FAREWELL IN FEBRUARY

I

Through the small window on the stair
As I leant out to take the air
At the slow-fading end of day,
I heard the thrushes sing and say :
This is the end of winter.

This is the end, I thought, although
The northward fields are rimmed with snow,
And like a thrush's breast the down
Is speckled o'er with white and brown ;
Though no sharp plough the furrow grooves,
Though still the seagulls' white-winged droves
Flurry above the inland plain—
Winter withdraws from earth again—
This is the end of winter.

Since then, I thought, I shall not see
New buds alight in every tree,

Nor watch the sun at evenfall
Put gold upon my bedroom wall,
And no more at this window lean
To feel the sweet air pressing in—
Here for a little while I'll rest
And mark the garden's every crest,
That in my mind when I am gone
Its birds and boughs may still live on.

II

This place that I'll not see again
Shall wear its seasons in my brain;
Clothed in fine weather it shall shine
Thorough what journeys may be mine,
Nor drought nor deluge shall destroy
What in my fancy I enjoy.
Here not a seed on barren ground
Shall fall, and not a grub be found.
All happy weathers, seasons, hours,
Entangled still with fruit and flowers,
In gay confusion shall display
The charms of Michaelmas or May.
Fresh leaves and blossoms I'll set in it
And plums shall ripened be next minute;

Through scarlet currants that appear
Like earrings in a lady's ear
Shall slant the beams of morning sun—
Next pinks breathe sweet and day be done .
There be the moon and there tiptoe
The stars among the branches go,
And that young jasmine by the wall
Shall grow a flowery waterfall.

So rich in crops, so quickly weeded,
Where never fork or hoe is needed,
This place I leave beneath grey skies
Shall be my spirit's paradise.

III

What once was there and what there never
Who from thought's thicket can dissever?
Through the green branches looking down
Into this Eden of my own,
Unchanging phantoms I shall see
Myself and you who walked with me,
Two skipping children long since grown,
A cat long dead and birds long flown,
And so substantial I shall find
The dreams that living leaves behind;

All hopes, all loves, all ecstasies
Stolen from life, I shall find these.
What memory cannot paint be sure
Fancy will fashion more secure.

Those woven boughs, that silken sky,
Regret nor winter will come nigh;
Beyond the reach of mortal grief
Its every shining flower and leaf;
Growing but fading not shall be
The span of its mortality,
And time's sad progress shall be stayed
By the perfection of a shade.

LOOKING AT THE STARS

Now, by night, while all is still,
Orion with a flaming heel,
Marches on the western hill :—
Constellations with him wheel

Westward, ever westward moving,
Many a hero, many a god,
Fierce in war and fierce in loving :—
Men in ancient times who trod

This strange planet knew and named
Their great deeds, proclaimed their glories,
While the white stars blinked and flamed :—
Shades of shades those men; but stories

Live when speaking lips are dumb :—
Is it their night-haunting breath
Across unnumbered ages come,
Breathes in my hair the chill of death ?

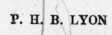
P. H. B. LYON

COMMUNION

At the waking of birds,
  In the hush of morning,
We whisper the words
  Of praise and repentance;
The sun from the East
  Stains pillar and chancel,
The voice of the priest
  Comes soft-toned and solemn;
And out in the world
  The first dews are trampled,
The dawn-mists are furled,
  The cows go from milking,
A cock crows loud
  From the farmyard midden;
But here in a cloud
  Of worship and silence
We keep the old tryst,
  We serve the commandment
Of Jesus the Christ;
  Desiring, receiving—
To the carol of birds,
  In a world just waking—
The comfortable words
  Of Jesus the Saviour.

P. B. H. LYON

" NOW TO BE STILL AND REST "

Now to be still and rest, while the heart
    remembers
    All that it learned and loved in the days long
        past,
To stoop and warm our hands at the fallen
    embers,
    Glad to have come to the long way's end at
        last.

Now to awake, and feel no regret at waking,
    Knowing the shadowy days are white again,
To draw our curtains and watch the slow dawn
        breaking
    Silver and grey on English field and lane.

Now to fulfil our dreams, in woods and meadows
    Treading the well-loved paths,—to pause and
        cry
" So, even so I remember it,"—seeing the
    shadows
    Weave on the distant hills their tapestry.

Now to rejoice in children and join their laughter,
  Tuning our hearts once more to the fairy
      strain,—
To hear our names on voices we love, and after
  Turn with a smile to sleep and our dreams
      again.

Then—with a newborn stength, the sweet rest
      over,
  Gladly to follow the great white road once
      more,
To work with a song on our lips and the heart of
      a lover,
  Building the city of peace on the wastes of war.

ENVOI

Earth puts her colours by,
And veils her in one whispering cloak of shadow;
Green goes from the meadow;
Red leaves and flowers and shining pools are
    shrouded;
A few stars sail upon a windy sky,
And the moon is clouded.

The delicate music, traced
In and out of the soft lights and the laughter,
Is hushed, round ledge and rafter
The last faint echoes into silence creeping:
The harp is mute, the violins encased,
And the singers sleeping.

So, now my songs are done,
Leave me to night awhile and the starlight gleam
    ing,
To silence and sweet dreaming,
Here where no music calls, no beauty shakes me;
Till in my heart the birds sing to the sun
And the new dawn wakes me.

292

ROSE MACAULAY

NEW YEAR 1918

Whatever the year brings, he brings nothing new,
For time, caught on the ancient wheel of change,
Spins round, and round, and round; and nothing
      is strange,
    Or shall amaze
Minkind, in whom the heritage of all days
Stirs suddenly, as dreams half remembered do.
Whatever the year brings, he brings nothing new.

    Pale, pale he stands,
Carrying world-old gifts in his cold hands—
    Winds, and the sky's keen blue
    Woods, and the wild cuckoo,
Lovers, and loveliness, and death, and life.
Does he hold Peace, the derelict babe of strife
    And of wan penury?
Will she ride in on the wash of the storming sea,
Be dropped at last by its ebb on the trampled
      sands,
    To lie there helplessly?

War's orphan, she,
And ungrown mother of wars yet to be,
She smiles and croons for a space between these
        two.
Whatever the year brings, he brings nothing new.

Dreams and desires and hopes does the year hold.
        Bad and good, tinsel and gold,
        Lying and true,
        One and all they are old, so old,
        They were dreamt and desired and told
By the first men swinging in trees by strong tails.
        Not till the last man fails,
        And the sun's fire pales,
Shall the embers of these flaming dreams be cold.
Whatever the year brings, he brings nothing new.

        Turn, turn the page!
It turns, and we, and the squirrel in his cage,
And the sun, and the moon, and the moon's salt
        tide;
        And the earth turns too.
As flies on the rim of a wheel we ride
        From age round to age;
And the dreams and the toys which make our
        pride

Are an old heritage,
Worn properties from some primeval stage
All curtained now from view . . .
Whatever the year brings, he brings nothing new.

Go through the door.
You shall find nothing that has not been before,
Nothing so bitter it will not be once more.
All this our sad estate was known of yore,
In old worlds red with pain,
Borne by hearts sullen and sick as ours, through
Desperate, forgotten, other winters, when
Tears fell, and hopes, and men,
And crowns and cities, and blood, on a trampled
plain,
And nations, and honour, and God, and always
rain . . .
And honour and hope and God rose up again,
And like trees nations grew . . .
Whatever the year brings, he brings nothing new.

Should some year suddenly bring something new,
We should grope as lost children without a clue.
We should drift all amazed through such a queer
And unimagined year.
Riding uncharted seas, a derelict crew,
Whistling in vain for the old winds that blew

From the old skies, we should seek far and near
    Some mark by which to steer,
And some known port, that we might sail thereto
    Black nightmare and blind fear
    Shall seize and hold him who
In some year suddenly finds something new.

ALL SOULS' DAY 1916

The men are black as the cursed night,
  Or brown as *café au lait*,
Or golden amber, like pale sherry,
  Or blind to the blowing day,
Or, for some ill deed they have wrought,
  Condemned to limp alway.

They talk with the tongues of aliens;
  They shake in the keen breeze.
(The keen breeze searches the chill bones
  Of Cambridge men, not these,
Of Cambridge men keeping their terms
  In trenches overseas;
And of colder Cambridge men who lie
  In No Man's Land at ease.)

    *   *   *   *

Like thieves about the grey city
  The brown men creep, afraid,
Creep down St. Edward's passage way,
  And lurk there in the shade,
As if they found no room to walk
  To-day, in King's Parade.

Yesterday was All Hallows',
   And bright with the saints' beams.
To-day the leaves blow down, blow down,
   Through tears the sun gleams.
And O, to-day the young men come,
   Washed on a drift of dreams.

There's a light whisper of laughter
   Down Trinity Street,
A flutter of gowns in the thronged Cury,
   And on Pease Hill beat,
Like waves striking a mist-drowned shore,
   An army of feet.

Cambridge town is carried and stormed,
   And the black, lame, and blind,
Creep perplexed through the blithe city
   That is grown gay and unkind. . . .

     *   *   *   *

The strange tide will ebb again
   Before the dawn star,
Ebb and drift, whispering
   Out beyond the bar,
Back to the shores (more near than France)
   Where the Cambridge men are.

The blacks will walk the empty streets,
   Securely at their ease;
They'll walk, gibbering black men's speech,
   'Twixt the Great Gate and Caius;
But ever they'll pale, as black men pale,
   A-wilting in the breeze,
To think how Cambridge called her own
   From beyond the bitter seas.

JOHN MASEFIELD

THE RACER

I saw the racer coming to the jump,
  Staring with fiery eyeballs as he rusht,
I heard the blood within his body thump,
  I saw him launch, I heard the toppings crusht.

And as he landed I beheld his soul
  Kindle, because, in front, he saw the Straight
With all its thousands roaring at the goal,
  He laughed, he took the moment for his mate.

Would that the passionate moods on which we
    ride
  Might kindle thus to oneness with the will;
Would we might see the end to which we stride,
  And feel, not strain, in struggle, only thrill.

And laugh like him and know in all our nerves
Beauty, the spirit, scattering dust and turves.

THE RIDER AT THE GATE

A windy night was blowing on Rome,
The cressets guttered on Cæsar's home,
The fish-boats, moored at the bridge, were
    breaking
The rush of the river to yellow foam.

The hinges whined to the shutters shaking,
When clip-clop-clep came a horse-hoof raking
The stones of the road at Cæsar's gate;
The spear-butts jarred at the guard's awaking.

" Who goes there? " said the guard at the gate.
" What is the news, that you ride so late? "
" News most pressing, that must be spoken
To Cæsar alone, and that cannot wait."

" The Cæsar sleeps; you must show a token
That the news suffice that he be awoken.
What is the news, and whence do you come?
For no light cause may his sleep be broken."

" Out of the dark of the sands I come,
From the dark of death, with news for Rome.
A word so fell that it must be uttered
Though it strike the soul of the Cæsar dumb."

Cæsar turned in his bed and muttered,
With a struggle for breath the lamp-flame
guttered;
Calpurnia heard her husband moan:
" The house is falling,
The beaten men come into their own."

" Speak your word," said the guard at the gate;
" Yes, but bear it to Cæsar straight,
Say, ' Your murderer's knives are honing,
Your killer's gang is lying in wait.'

" Out of the wind that is blowing and moaning,
Through the city palace and the country loaning,
I cry, ' For the world's sake, Cæsar, beware,
And take this warning as my atoning.

" ' Beware of the Court, of the palace stair,
Of the downcast friend who speaks so fair,
Keep from the Senate, for Death is going
On many men's feet to meet you there.'

" I, who am dead, have ways of knowing
Of the crop of death that the quick are sowing.
I, who was Pompey, cry it aloud
From the dark of death, from the wind blowing.

" I, who was Pompey, once was proud,
Now I lie in the sand without a shroud;
I cry to Cæsar out of my pain,
' Cæsar, beware, your death is vowed.' "

The light grew grey on the window-pane,
The windcocks swung in a burst of rain,
The window of Cæsar flung unshuttered,
The horse-hoofs died into wind again.

Cæsar turned in his bed and muttered,
With a struggle for breath the lamp-flame
          guttered;
Calpurnia heard her husband moan:
          " The house is falling,
The beaten men come into their own."

HAROLD MONRO

UNKNOWN COUNTRY

Here in this other world, they come and go
With easy dream-like movements to and fro.
They stare through lovely eyes, yet do not seek
An answering gaze, or that a man should speak.
Had I a load of gold, and should I come
Bribing their friendship, and to buy a home,
They would stare harder and would slightly
    frown :
I am a stranger from the distant town.

Oh, with what patience I have tried to win
The favour of the hostess of the Inn !
Have I not offered toast on frothing toast
Looking toward the melancholy host ;
Praised the old wall-eyed mare to please the
    groom ;
Laughed to the laughing maid and fetched her
    broom ;
Stood in the background not to interfere
When the cool ancients frolicked at their beer ;

Talked only in my turn, and made no claim
For recognition or by voice or name,
Content to listen, and to watch the blue
Or grey of eyes, or what good hands can do?

Sun-freckled lads, who at the dusk of day
Stroll through the village with a scent of hay
Clinging about you from the windy hill,
Why do you keep your secret from me still?
You loiter at the corner of the street;
I in the distance silently entreat.
I know too well I'm city soiled, but then
So are to-day ten million other men.
My heart is true : I've neither will nor charms
To lure away your maidens from your arms.
Trust me a little. Must I always stand
Lonely, a stranger from an unknown land?
There is a riddle here. Though I'm more wise
Than you, I cannot read your simple eyes.
I find the meaning of their gentle look
More difficult than any learned book.
I pass : perhaps a moment you may chaff
My walk, and so dismiss me with a laugh.
I come : you all, most grave and most polite,
Stand silent first, then wish me calm Good-Night.

When I go back to town someone will say :
" I think that stranger must have gone away."
And " Surely ! " someone else will then reply.
Meanwhile, within the dark of London, I
Shall, with my forehead resting on my hand,
Not cease remembering your distant land ;
Endeavouring to reconstruct aright
How some treed hill has looked in evening light ;
Or be imagining the blue of skies
Now as in heaven, now as in your eyes ;
Or in my mind confusing looks or words
Of yours with dawnlight, or the song of birds :
Not able to resist, not even keep
Myself from hovering near you in my sleep :
You still as callous to my thought and me
As flowers to the purpose of the bee.

THISTLEDOWN

This might have been a place for sleep,
But, as from that small hollow there
Hosts of bright thistledown begin
Their dazzling journey through the air,
An idle man can only stare.

They grip their withered edge of stalk
In brief excitement for the wind;
They hold a breathless final talk,
And when their filmy cables part
One almost hears a little cry.

Some cling together while they wait,
And droop and gaze and hesitate,
But others leap along the sky,
Or circle round and calmly choose
The gust they know they ought to use;

While some in loving pairs will glide,
Or watch the others as they pass,
Or rest on flowers in the grass,

Or circle through the shining day
Like silvery butterflies at play.

Some catch themselves to every mound,
Then lingeringly and slowly move
As if they knew the precious ground
Were opening for their fertile love :
They almost try to dig, they need
So much to plant their thistle-seed.

JOHN MIDDLETON MURRY

SERENITY

I ask no more for wonders : let me be
At peace within my heart, my fever stilled
By the calm circuit of the year fulfilled,
Autumn to follow summer in the tree
Of my new-ordered being. Silently
My leaves shall on the unfretting earth be spilled,
The pride be slowly scattered that shall gild
A windless triumph of serenity.

Vex me no more with dreams ; the tortured mind
Hath turned and rent the dreamer. Foreordain
My motions, and my seasons solemn lead
Each to his own perfection whence declined
Their measured sequence promise shall contain,
And my late-opened husk let fall a seed.

TRAIN JOURNEY

For what cause? To what end?
Into what nameless disaster speeding
Through a twilight cavern of space unheeding,
Through vapours of tears, with a numb heart
    bleeding,
Torn from what friend?

Cause there is none, nor friend;
Nor was that joy from which I parted,
But only what is no longer, yet departed
Its voice rings golden to me broken-hearted,
Saying, There is no end.

ROBERT NICHOLS

NIGHT RHAPSODY

How beautiful it is to wake at night,
When over all there reigns the ultimate spell
Of complete silence, darkness absolute,
To feel the world, tilted on axle-tree,
In slow gyration, with no sensible sound,
Unless to ears of unimagined beings,
Resident incorporeal or stretched
In vigilance of ecstasy among
Ethereal paths and the celestial maze.
The rumour of our onward course now brings
A steady rustle, as of some strange ship
Darkling with soundless sail all set and amply
  filled
By volume of an ever-constant air,
At fullest night, through seas forever calm,
Swept lovely and unknown forever on.

How beautiful it is to wake at night,
Embalmed in darkness watchful, sweet and still,

As is the brain's mood flattered by the swim
Of currents circumvolent in the void,
To lie quite still and to become aware
Of the dim light cast by nocturnal skies
On a dim earth beyond the window-ledge,
So, isolate from the friendly company
Of the huge universe which turns without,
To brood apart in calm and joy awhile
Until the spirit sinks and scarcely knows
Whether self is, or if self only is,
For ever. . . .

How beautiful to wake at night,
Within the room grown strange, and still, and
    sweet,
And live a century while in the dark
The dripping wheel of silence slowly turns,
To watch the window open on the night,
A dewy silent deep where nothing stirs,
And, lying thus, to feel dilate within
The press, the conflict, and the heavy pulse
Of incommunicable sad ecstasy,
Growing until the body seems outstretched
In perfect crucifixion on the arms
Of a cross pointing from last void to void,
While the heart dies to a mere midway spark.

All happiness thou holdest, happy night,
For such as lie awake and feel dissolved
The peaceful spice of darkness and the cool
Breath hither blown from the ethereal flowers
That mist thy fields! O happy, happy wounds,
Conditioned by existence in humanity,
That have such powers to heal them! Slow
    sweet sighs
Torn from the bosom, silent wails, the birth
Of such long-treasured tears as pain the eyes,
Who, waking, hears the divine solicitudes
Of midnight with ineffable purport charged.

How beautiful it is to wake at night,
Another night, in darkness yet more still,
Save when the myriad leaves on full-fledged
    boughs,
Filled rather by the perfume's wandering flood
Than by dispansion of the still sweet air,
Shall from the furthest utter silences
In glimmering secrecy have gathered up
An host of whisperings and scattered sighs,
To loose at last a sound as of the plunge
And lapsing seethe of some Pacific wave,
Which, risen from the star-thronged outer
    troughs,

Rools in to wreathe with circling foam away
The flutter of the golden moths that haunt
The star's one glimmer daggered on wet sands.

So beautiful it is to wake at night !
Imagination, loudening with the surf
Of the midsummer wind among the boughs,
Gathers my spirit from the haunts remote
Of faintest silence and the shades of sleep,
To bear me on the summit of her wave
Beyond known shores, beyond the mortal edge
Of thought terrestial, to hold me poised
Above the frontiers of infinity,
To which in the full reflux of the wave
Come soon I must, bubble of solving foam,
Borne to those other shores—now never mine
Save for a hovering instant, short as this
Which now sustains me ere I be drawn back—
To learn again, and wholly learn, I trust,
How beautiful it is to wake at night.

ALFRED NOYES

THE SHADOW

A shadow leaned over me, whispering, in the
      darkness,
      Thoughts without sound—
Sorrowful thoughts that filled me with helpless
      wonder
      And held me bound.

Sadder than memory, sharp as remorse, in the
      quiet
      Before I slept,
The whisper I heard of the one implacable
      Shadow,
      And my heart wept.

" Day by day, in your eyes, the light grows
      dimmer,
      With the joy you have sung.
You knew it would go; but, ah, when you knew
      it and sang it
      Your heart was young;

" And a year to you, then was an age; but now,"
                said the Shadow,
        Malignant and cold,
" The light and the colour are fading, the ecstasy
                dying,
        It is time to grow old."

Oh, I could have borne the worst that he had to
                tell me,
        Lost youth, age, death;
But he turned to breathe on the quiet heart sleep-
                ing beside me
        The same cold breath.

And there by the throat I grappled him. " Let
                me bear all of it.
        Let her dream on."
Soundlessly, shadow with shadow, we wrestled
                together,
        Till the grey dawn.

THE LAST OF THE BOOKS

Is it too strange to think
    That, when all life at last from earth is gone,
And round the sun's pale blink
    Our desolate planet wheels its ice and stone,
Housed among storm-proof walls there yet may
      abide
    Defying long the venoms of decay,
A still dark throng of books, dumb books of song
    And tenderest fancies born of youth and May.

A quiet remembering host,
    Out-living the poor dust that gave them birth,
Unvisited by even a wandering ghost,
    But treasuring still the music of our earth,
In little fading hieroglyphs they shall bear
    Through death and night, the legend of our
      Spring,
And how the lilac scented the bright air
    When hearts throbbed warm, and lips could
      kiss and sing.

And, ere that record fail,
   Strange voyagers from a mightier planet come
On wingèd ships that through the void can sail
   And gently alight upon our ancient home;
Strange voices echo, and strange flares explore,
   Strange hands, with curious weapons, burst
      these bars,
Lift the brown volumes to the light once more,
   And bear their stranger secrets through the
      stars.

SEAGULLS ON THE SERPENTINE

Memory, out of the mist, in a long slow ripple
    Breaks, blindly, against the shore.
The mist has buried the town in its own oblivion.
    This, this is the sea once more.

Mist—mist—brown mist; but a sense in the air of
    snowflakes!
    I stand where the ripples die,
Lift up an arm and wait, till my lost ones know
    me,
    Wheel overhead, and cry.

Salt in the eyes, and the seagulls, mewing and
    swooping,
    Snatching the bread from my hand;
Brushing my hand with their breasts, in swift
    caresses
    To show that they understand.

Oh, why are you so afraid? We are all of us
    exiles!
    Wheel back in your clamorous rings!
We have all of us lost the sea, and we all
    remember.
    But you—have wings.

ON REMBRANDT'S PORTRAIT OF A RABBI

He has thought and suffered, but without a cry.
  The wan-hope of this wise old face appears
  To watch, with eyes that hide their own deep
      tears,
The generations hurrying down to die;
For he can see, beyond our midnight sky
  New griefs arising with the unborn years;
  And, brooding on the riddle of things, he bears
His load of thought, in dreadful innocency.
Children have nestled to him; but all are flown.
  He awaits their homing wings, as old men do
    Across this world's bewildering surge and
        roar.
An envoy of the Eternal and Unknown;
  An alien to all pride; he faces you,
    In simplest brotherhood, and desires no
        more.

A FOREST SONG

Who would be a king
That can sit in the sun and sing?
Nay. I have a kingdom of my own.
A fallen oak-tree is my throne.
> *Then pluck the strings and tell me true*
> *If Cæsar in his glory knew*
> *The worlds he lost in sun and dew.*

Who would be a queen
That sees what my love hath seen?—
The blood of myriads vainly shed
To make one royal ruby red!
> *Then, tell me, music, why the great*
> *For quarrelling trumpets abdicate*
> *This quick, this absolute estate.*

Nay. Who would sing in heaven
Among the choral Seven,
That hears, as Love and I have heard,
The whole sky listening to one bird?
> *And where's the ruby, tell me where,*
> *Whose crimsons for one breath compare*
> *With this wild rose which all may share?*

WILFRED OWEN

Killed in Action 1918

FUTILITY

Move him into the sun—
Gently its touch awoke him once,
At home, whispering of fields unsown.
Always it woke him, even in France,
Until this morning and this snow.
If anything might rouse him now
The kind old sun will know.

Think how it wakes the seeds—
Woke, once, the clays of a cold star.
Are limbs so dear-achieved, are sides
Full-nerved,—still warm,—too hard to stir?
Was it for this the clay grew tall?
O what made fatuous sunbeams toil
To break earth's sleep at all?

SPRING OFFENSIVE

Halted against the shade of a last hill,
They fed, and, lying easy, were at ease
And, finding comfortable chests and knees
Carelessly slept. But many there stood still
To face the stark, blank sky beyond the ridge,
Knowing their feet had come to the end of the
      world.

Marvelling they stood, and watched the long
      grass swirled
By the May breeze, murmurous with wasp and
      midge,
For though the summer oozed into their veins
Like the injected drug for their bones' pains,
Sharp on their souls hung the imminent line of
      grass,
Fearfully flashed the sky's mysterious glass.

Hour after hour they ponder in the warm field—
And the valley far behind, where the buttercups
Had blessed with gold their slow boots coming up.

Where even the little brambles would not yield,
But clutched and clung to them like sorrowing
    hands;
They breathe like trees unstirred.

Till like a cold gust thrilled the little word
At which each body and its soul begird
And tighten them for battle. No alarms
Of bugles, no high flags, no clamorous haste—
Only a lift and flare of eyes that faced
The sun, like a friend with whom their love is
    done.
O larger shone that smile against the sun,—
Mightier than his whose bounty these have
    spurned.

So, soon they topped the hill, and raced together
Over an open stretch of herb and heather
Exposed. And instantly the whole sky burned
With fury against them; and soft sudden cups
Opened in thousands for their blood; and the
    green slopes
Chasmed and steepened sheer to infinite space.

Of them who running on that last high place
Leapt to swift unseen bullets, or went up

On the hot blast and fury of hell's upsurge,
Or plunged and fell away past this world's verge,
Some say God caught them even before they fell.

But what say such as from existence' brink
Ventured but drave too swift to sink.
The few who rushed in the body to enter hell,
And there out-fiending all its fiends and flames
With superhuman inhumanities,
Long-famous glories, immemorial shames—
And crawling slowly back, have by degrees
Regained cool peaceful air in wonder—
Why speak they not of comrades that went
    under?

ANTHEM FOR DOOMED YOUTH

What passing-bells for these who die as cattle?
  Only the monstrous anger of the guns.
  Only the stuttering rifles' rapid rattle
Can patter out their hasty orisons.
No mockeries for them; no prayers nor bells,
Nor any voice of mourning save the choirs,—
The shrill, demented choirs of wailing shells;
And bugles calling for them from sad shires.

What candles may be held to speed them all?
  Not in the hands of boys, but in their eyes
Shall shine the holy glimmer of good-byes.
  The pallor of girls' brows shall be their pall;
Their flowers the tenderness of patient minds,
And each slow dusk a drawing-down of blinds.

THE SEND-OFF

Down the close, darkening lanes they sang their
    way
To the siding shed,
And lined the train with faces grimly gay.

Their breasts were stuck all white with wreath
    and spray
As men's are, dead.

Dull porters watched them, and a casual tramp
Stood staring hard,
Sorry to miss them from the upland camp.
Then, unmoved, signals nodded, and a lamp
Winked to the guard.

So secretly, like wrongs hushed up, they went.
They were not ours :
We never heard to which front these were sent.

Nor there if they yet mock what women meant
Who gave them flowers.

Shall they return to beatings of great bells
In wild trainloads ?
A few, a few, too few for drums and yells,
May creep back, silent, to still vintage wells
Up half-known roads.

GREATER LOVE

Red lips are not so red
  As the stained stones kissed by the English
    dead.
Kindness of wooed and wooer
Seems shame to their love pure.
O Love, your eyes lose lure
  When I behold eyes blinded in my stead !

Your slender attitude
  Trembles not exquisite like limbs knife-skewed,
Rolling and rolling there
Where God seems not to care ;
Till the fierce love they bear
  Cramps them in death's extreme decrepitude.

Your voice sings not so soft,—
  Though even as wind murmuring through
    raftered loft,—

Your dear voice is not dear,
Gentle, and evening clear,
As theirs whom none now hear
  Now earth has stopped their piteous mouths
      that coughed.

Heart, you were never hot,
  Nor large, nor full like hearts made great with
      shot;
And though your hand be pale,
Paler are all which trail
Your cross through flame and hail:
  Weep, you may weep, for you may touch them
      not.

J. D. C. PELLOW

AFTER LONDON

London Bridge is broken down;
  Green is the grass of Ludgate Hill;
I know a farmer in Camden Town
  Killed a brock by Pentonville.

I have heard my grandam tell
  How some thousand years ago
Houses stretched from Camberwell
  Right to Highbury and Bow.

Down by Shadwell's golden meads
  Tall ships' masts would stand as thick
As the pretty tufted reeds
  That the Wapping children pick.

All the kings from end to end
  Of all the world paid tribute then,
And meekly on the knees would bend
  To the King of Englishmen.

Thinks I while I dig my plot,
  What if your grandam's tales be true?
Thinks I, be they true or not,
  What's the odds to a fool like you?

Thinks I, while I smoke my pipe
  Here beside the tumbling Fleet,
Apples drop when they are ripe,
  And when they drop they are most sweet.

ECLOGA VIRGILIANA

DENIS :

There is a hush in the air, in the paling skies,
Stirred only by a lapwing's desolate call,
And, " see the smoke from far-off chimneys rise
And from the high hills larger shadows fall."

MICHAEL :

Oh, could you find no fair words of your own?
Into the evening's beauty must you drag,
To break, like that sad bird, its tranquil tone,
Some melancholy, sweet, Virgilian tag?

DENIS :

Ay, sweet and true, and therefore readily came
Those words to greet and crown this loveliness.

MICHAEL :

But hard upon the utterance of that name
Thoughts, heavy and disturbing, crowd and press

351

Into my foolish, easily-saddened mind,
And break the rare and brief serenity,
So hard in these tempestuous days to find
And harder still to win—To think that he,
In a like time, as troubled, and as ripe
To fall and rot, dreaming an age of gold
Revolved again, of true Saturnian type,
Half-seriously and all unwittingly, told
In a courtly song the blessed babe that smiled
With its first awful breath of earthly air,
And never thought or dreamed that heavenly
    child
More than an idle dream, impossibly fair.

DENIS :

Strange irony, to think of Virgil turned
A prophet, almost canonised a saint,
For that rococo pastoral we have learned
To find so full of cold court-flattery's taint.

MICHAEL :

Perhaps the Church, more wise than we, dis
    cerned
Behind those borrowed ornaments, so crude

And childish, as we think now, burning dim
A gentle spirit akin to theirs, who viewed
With sad and longing eyes the clouded rim
Of his distracted world, and eased his heart,
That saw no hope or peace there, in a song
Coloured and formed with fond, half-playful art.
In such a world as Virgil's, such a time,
But darker still, and riper to decay,
And more than ripe, I fashion into rhyme
The longing of my god-forsaken day.
But here's the bitter thought, that when I read
The frozen heaven for signs, the blasted earth,
All round I see the bitter insistent need,
But promise nowhere of so bright a birth
As Virgil sang.

DENIS :

      Yet never saw, for we
Must hope, though we may never hope to see.
But come, put off awhile your sadness, here
Is our inn-window, glowing with homely cheer.

FRANK PREWETT

VOICES OF WOMEN

Met ye my love?
Ye might in France have met him;
He has a wooing smile,
Who sees cannot forget him!
Met ye my love?
—We shared full many a mile.

Saw ye my love?
In lands far-off he has been,
With his yellow-tinted hair,—
In Egypt such ye have seen,
Ye knew my love?
—I was his brother there.

Heard ye my love?
My love ye must have heard,
For his voice when he will
Tinkles like cry of a bird;
Heard ye my love?—
—We sang on a Grecian hill.

Behold your love,
And how shall I forget him,
His smile, his hair, his song;
Alas, no maid shall get him
For all her love,
Where he sleeps a million strong.

Their leaves are stripped away
By savage winds at play,
And the groaning trees ask not the cause;
The merry trilling bird
That I rejoicing heard
In the snow lies dead with upthrust claws.

The kindly skies of blue
Are overclouded too,
And the clouds, no more than skies, are glad;
The huddling, frightened sheep
In sheltered corners creep,
For they fear the night-time wet and sad.

In secret, women cry,
Though soft abed they lie,
For they who buy love find it sour;
While madness roams the streets
And howls at all he meets,
Since the loved and mad have each his hour.

Sure if a God there be,
He rides too high to see
In his vaunted world the pouring tears,
Or, floating there aloft,
Is settled much too soft
In His cloud to heed the shrieks and jeers.

The blind fates take their way,
We resist our little day,
And are ground in mud beneath the mire;
The fates are ignorant
As we, and what is meant
Shall not know till cleansing come with fire.

J. B. PRIESTLEY

AT A NIGHT CLUB

The young men shouted with the band
And pranced their partners across the floor,
Yet when they had done, I saw them stand
A moment—dubious in Elsinore.

OVERHEARD

Somewhere past Sirius, shade called to shade :
  " Well, any gossip? Something new, I trust? "
" Not much. They say that solar god has made
  Some quite amusing things out of his dust."

J. B. PRIESTLEY

THE OLD MAN AND THE NEWSPAPER

Daylong he seems to read, but as he peers
  At fading print, the sheet becomes a glass,
Wherein are mirrored ghosts that smile and pass,
  And lovely faces, dust these forty years.

J. B. PRIESTLEY

" Æ "

A shepherd, having left the hills to roam,
   Sees from afar the cities of great kings,
And so returns enraptured to his home :—
   A man apart—who stammers golden things.

V. SACKVILLE-WEST

TUSCANY

Cisterns and stones; the fig-tree in the wall
Casts down her shadow, ashen as her boughs
Across the road, across the thick white dust.
Down from the hill the slow white oxen crawl,
Dragging the purple waggon heaped with must,
With scarlet tassels on their milky brows,
Gentle as evening moths. Beneath the yoke
Lounging against the shaft they fitful strain
To draw the waggon on its creaking spoke,
And all the vineyard folk
With staves and shouldered tools surround the
    wain.
The wooden shovels take the purple stain,
The dusk is heavy with the wine's warm load;
Here the long sense of classic measure cures
The spirit weary of its difficult pain;
Here the old Bacchic piety endures,
Here the sweet legends of the world remain.

Homeric waggons lumbering the road;
Virgilian litanies among the bine;
Pastoral sloth of flocks beneath the pine;
The swineherd watching, propped upon his goad,
Under the chestnut trees the rootling swine,—
Who could so stand, and see this evening fall,
This calm of husbandry, this redolent tilth,
This terracing of hills, this vintage wealth,
Without the pagan sanity of blood
Mounting his veins in young and tempered
    health?
Who could so stand, and watch processional
The vintners, herds, and flocks in dusty train
Wend through the golden evening to regain
The terraced farm and trodden threshing floor
Where late the flail
Tossed high the maize in scud of gritty ore,
And lies half-buried in the heap of grain,—
Who could so watch, and not forget the rack
Of wills worn thin and thought become too frail,
Nor roll the centuries back
And feel the sinews of his soul grow hale,
And know himself for Rome's inheritor?

BEE-MASTER

I have known honey from the Syrian hills
Stored in cool jars; the wild acacia there
On the rough terrace where the locust shrills
Tosses her spindrift on the ringing air.
Narcissus bares his nectarous perianth
In white and golden tabard to the sun,
And while the workers rob the amaranth
Or scarlet windflower low among the stone,
Practical and intent upon their crops,
The Syrian queens mate in the high hot day
Rapt visionaries of creative fray;
Soar from their fecund ecstasy alone,
And, through the blazing ether, drops
Like a small thunderbolt the vindicated drone.
But this is the bee-master's reckoning
In England. Walk among the hives and hear.

Forget not bees in winter, though they sleep.
For winter's big with summer in her womb,
And when you plant your rose-trees, plant them
   deep,

371

Having regard to bushes all aflame,
And see the dusky promise of their bloom
In small red shoots, and let each redolent name—
Tuscany, Crested Cabbage, Cottage Maid—
Load with full June November's dank repose,
See the kind cattle drowsing in the shade,
And hear the bee about his amorous trade
Brown in the gipsy crimson of the rose.

In February, if the days be clear,
The waking bee, still drowsy on the wing,
Will sense the opening of another year
And blunder out to seek another spring.
Crashing through winter sunlight's pallid gold
His clumsiness sets catkins on the willow
Ashake like lambs' tails in the early fold,
Dusting with pollen all his brown and yellow,
But when the rimy afternoon turns cold
And undern squalls buffet the chilly fellow,
He'll seek the hive's warm waxen welcoming
And set about the chambers' classic mould.

And then, pell-mell, his harvest follows swift,
Blossom and borage, lime and balm and clover,
On Downs the thyme, on cliffs the scantling
    thrift,

Everywhere bees go racing with the hours,
For every bee becomes a drunken lover,
Standing upon his head to sup the flowers,
All over England, from Northumbrian coasts,
To the wild sea-pink blown on Devon rocks.
Over the merry southern gardens, over
The grey-green bean-fields, round the Sussex
  oasts,
Through the frilled spires of cottage hollyhocks,
Go the big brown fat bees, and blunder in
Where dusky spears of sunlight cleave the barn,
And seek the sun again, and storm the whin,
And in the warm meridian solitude
Hum in the heather round the moorland tarn.
Look, too, when summer hatches out the brood,
In tardy May or early June,
And the young queens are strong in the cocoon,
Watch, if the days be warm,
The flitting of the migratory swarm.
Follow, for if beyond your sight they stray
Your bees are lost, and you must take your
  way
Homeward disconsolate, but if you be at hand
Then you may take your bees on strangers' land.
Have your skep ready, drowse them with your
  smoke,

Whether they cluster on the handy bough
Or in the difficult hedge, be nimble now
For bees are captious folk
And quick to turn against the lubber's touch,
But if you shake them to their wicker hutch
Firmly, and turn towards the hive your skep,
Into the hive the clustered thousands stream,
Mounting the little slatted sloping step,
A ready colony, queen, workers, drones,
Patient to build again the waxen thrones
For younger queens, and all the chambered cells
For lesser brood, and all the immemorial scheme.

And still they labour, though the hand of man
Inscrutable and ravaging descend,
Pillaging in their citadels,
Defeating wantonly their provident plan,
Making havoc of their patient hoard;
Still start afresh, not knowing to what end,
Not knowing to what ultimate reward,
Or what new ruin of their garnered hive
The senseless god in man will send.
Still their blind stupid industry will strive,
Constructing for destruction pitiably,
That still their unintelligible lord
May reap his wealth from their calamity.

MAKING CIDER

I saw within the wheelwright's shed
The big round cartwheels, blue and red;
A plough with blunted share;
A blue tin jug; a broken chair;
And paint in trial patchwork square
Slapped up against the wall;
The lumber of the wheelwright's trade,
And tools on benches neatly laid,
The brace, the adze, the awl;

And, framed within the latticed panes,
Above the cluttered sill,
Saw rooks upon the stubble hill
Seeking forgotten grains;

And all the air was sweet and shrill
With juice of apples heaped in skips,
Fermenting, rotten, soft with bruise,
And all the yard was strewn with pips,
Discarded pulp, and wrung-out ooze,

That ducks with rummaging flat bill
Searched through beside the cider press
To gobble in their greediness.

The young men strained upon the crank
To wring the last reluctant inch.
They laughed together, fair and frank,
And threw their loins across the winch.
A holiday from field and dung,
From plough and harrow, scythe and spade,
To dabble in another trade,
To crush the pippins in the slats,
And see that in the little vats
An extra pint was wrung;

While round about the worthies stood,
Profuse in comment, praise or blame,
Content the press should be of wood,
Advising rum, decrying wheat,
And black strong sugar makes it sweet,
But still resolved, with maundering tongue,
That cider could not be the same
As once when they were young;
But still the young contemptuous men
Laughed kindly at their old conceit,
And strained upon the crank again.

Now barrels ranged in portly line
Mature through winter's sleep,
Aping the leisured sloth of wine
That dreams by Tiber or by Rhine,
Mellowing slow and deep;
But keen and cold the northern nights
Sharpen the quiet yard,
And sharp like no rich southern wine
The tang of cider bites;
For here the splintered stars and hard
Hold England in a frosty guard,
Orion and the Pleiades,
Above the wheelwright's shed,
And Sirius resting on the trees
While all the village snores abed.

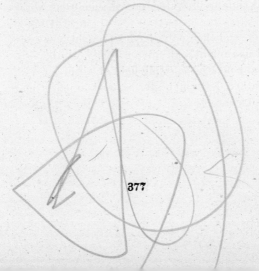

EVENING

When little lights in little ports come out,
Quivering down through water with the stars,
And all the fishing-fleet of slender spars
Range at their moorings, veer with tides about;

When race of wind is stilled and sails are furled,
And underneath our single riding-light
The curve of black-ribbed deck gleams palely
    white
And slumbrous waters pool a slumbrous world—

Then, and then only, have I thought how sweet
Old age might sink upon a windy youth,
Quiet beneath the riding-light of truth,
Weathered through storms, and gracious in re-
    treat.

V. SACKVILLE-WEST

SAILING SHIPS

Lying on Downs above the wrinkling bay
I with the kestrels shared the cleanly day,
The candid day; wind-shaven, brindled turf;
Tall cliffs; and long sea-line of marbled surf
From Cornish Lizard to the Kentish Nore
Lipping the bulwarks of the English shore,
While many a lovely ship below sailed by
On unknown errand, kempt and leisurely;
And after each, oh, after each, my heart
Fled forth, as, watching from the Downs apart,
I shared with ships good joys and fortunes wide
That might befall their beauty and their pride;

Shared first with them the blessèd void repose
Of oily days at sea, when only rose
The porpoise's slow wheel to break the sheen
Of satin water indolently green,
When for'ard the crew, caps tilted over eyes,
Lay heaped on deck; slept; murmured; smoked;
    threw dice;

The sleepy summer days; the summer nights
(The coast pricked out with rings of harbour-
    lights)
The motionless nights, the vaulted nights of June
When high in the cordage drifts the entangled
    moon,
And blocks go knocking, and the sheets go
    slapping,
And lazy swells against the sides come lapping;
And summer mornings off red Devon rocks,
Faint inland bells at dawn and crowing cocks.
Shared swifter days, when headlands into ken
Trod grandly; threatened; and were lost again,
Old fangs along the battlemented coast;
And followed still my ship, when winds were most
Night-purified, and, lying steeply over,
She fled the wind as flees a girl her lover,
Quickened by that pursuit for which she fretted,
Her temper by the contest proved and whetted;
Wild stars swept overhead; her lofty spars
Reared to a ragged heaven sown with stars
As leaping out from narrow English ease
She faced the roll of long Atlantic seas;

Her captain then was I, I was her crew,
The mind that laid her course, the wake she drew,

The waves that rose against her bows, the
    gales,—
Nay; I was more : I was her very sails
Rounded before the wind, her eager keel,
Her straining mast-heads, her responsive wheel,
Her pennon stiffened like a swallow's wing;
Yes, I was all her slope and speed and swing,
Whether by yellow lemons and blue sea
She dawdled through the isles off Thessaly,
Or saw the palms like sheaves of scimitars
On desert's verge below the sunset bars,
Or passed the girdle of the planet where
The Southern Cross looks over to the Bear,
And strayed, cool Northerner beneath strange
    skies,
Flouting the lure of tropic estuaries,
Down that long coast, and saw Magellan's Clouds
    arise.

And some that beat up Channel homeward-bound
I watched, and wondered what they might have
    found,
What alien ports enriched their teeming hold
With crates of fruit or bars of unwrought gold?
And thought how London clerks with paper-clips
Had filed the bills of lading of those ships,

Clerks that had never seen the embattled sea,
But wrote down jettison and barratry,
Perils, Adventures, and the Act of God,
Having no vision of such wrath flung broad;
Wrote down with weary and accustomed pen
The classic dangers of sea-faring men;
And wrote " Restraint of Princes," and " the
    acts
Of the King's Enemies," as vacant facts,
Blind to the ambushed seas, the encircling roar
Of angry nations foaming into war.

TRIO

So well she knew them both ! yet as she came
Into the room, and heard their speech
Of tragic meshes knotted with her name,
And saw them, foes, but meeting each with each
Closer than friends, souls bared through enmity,
Beneath their startled gaze she thought that she
Broke as the stranger on their conference,
And left them as she stole abashed from thence.

FULL MOON

She was wearing the coral taffeta trousers
Someone had brought her from Ispahan,
And the little gold coat with pomegranate blos-
    soms,
And the coral-hafted feather fan;
But she ran down a Kentish lane in the moon-
    light,
And skipped in the pool of the moon as she ran.

She cared not a rap for all the big planets,
For Betelgeuse or Aldebaran,
And all the big planets cared nothing for her,
That small impertinent charlatan;
But she climbed on a Kentish stile in the moon-
    light,
And laughed at the sky through the sticks of her
    fan.

SIEGFRIED SASSOON

EARLY CHRONOLOGY

Slowly the daylight left our listening faces.

*　　　　*　　　　*

　Professor Brown with level baritone
Discoursed into the dusk.
　　　　　　　　Five thousand years
He guided us through scientific spaces
Of excavated History; till the lone
Roads of research grew blurred; and in our ears
Time was the rumoured tongues of vanished
　　races,
And Thought a chartless Age of Ice and stone.

*　　　　*　　　　*

The story ended.　Then the darkened air
Flowered as he lit his pipe; an aureole glowed
Enwreathed with smoke; the moment's match-
　　light showed
His rosy face, broad brow, and smooth grey hair,
Backed by the crowded book-shelves.

              In his wake
An archæologist began to make
Assumptions about aqueducts (he quoted
Professor Sandstorm's book); and soon they
    floated
Through desiccated forests; mangled myths;
And argued easily round megaliths.

        *   *   *

Beyond the college garden something glinted;
A copper moon climbed clear above the trees.
Some Lydian coin? . . . Professor Brown agrees
That copper coins *were* in that culture minted;
But, as her whitening way aloft she took,
I thought she had a pre-dynastic look.

SOLAR ECLIPSE

Observe these blue solemnities of sky
Offering for the academes of after-ages
A mythologic welkin freaked with white !

Listen : one tiny tinkling rivulet
Accentuates the super-sultry stillness
That drones on ripening landscapes which imply
Serene Parnassus plagued with amorous goats.

*   *   *

Far down the vale Apollo has pursued
The noon-bedazzled nymph whose hunted heart
Holds but the trampling panic whence it fled.
And now the heavens are piled with darkening
        trouble
And counter-march of clouds that troop intent
Fire-crested into conflict.

                    Daphne turns
At the wood's edge in bronze and olive gloom :
Sickness assails the sun, whose blazing disc

Dwindles : the Eden of those auburn slopes
Lours in the tarnished copper of eclipse.

Yet virgin, in her god-impelled approach
To Græco-Roman ravishment, she waits
While the unsated python slides to crush
Her lust-eluding fleetness. Envious Jove
Rumbles Olympus. All the classic world
Leans breathless toward the legend she creates.

From thunderous vapour smites the immortal
    beam . . .
Then, crowned with fangs of foliage, flames the
    god.

*   *   *

Apollo! . . . Up the Autumn valley echoes
A hollow shout from nowhere. Daphne's limbs
Lapse into laureldom : green-shadowed flesh
Writhes arborescent : glamour obscures her gaze
With blind and bossed distortion. She escapes.

FANTASIA ON A WITTELSBACH
ATMOSPHERE

Drab drugget paths protect these polished floors
From tourist-soled attrition. Guide-book phrases
Co-ordinate fatigued and baffled brains
With mute ex-regal affluence. Simpering faces
Exposed in state-saloons and corridors
Survive the modes of soporific reigns.

A baton, and a battle (was it Blenheim ?)
Respectfully remote; the steed curvetting
Beneath his flushed Elector : what's the betting
He failed ? . . . no gouty poet lives to pen him
Campaign-concluding odes. Mark, too, the mien
(Obese in ermine, sceptred and serene,)
Of goggling Max Augustus ! Where's the Court
That equerried his jinks down aisles of green
To chevy stags in sycophantic sport?

Nevertheless, while strolling past such glories,
(Van Dyck to Winterhalter; stiff brocade
And powder, to frock-coats and whiskered smiles,)

My spirit shares with monarchismal Tories
The Fairy-Tale of Flunkeydom, displayed
In feudal relicry of centuried styles.
  My sympathy for Soviets notwithstanding—
(Dare one deplore the dullness of Democracy?)
I am touched, I am enticed, by super-lavish
Expense; half-cultured coxcomb Kings com-
      manding
In palacefuls the trappings of Autocracy,
With all their country's coffers ripe to ravish!

*   *   *

Outside, sham Renaissance façades evade
Modernity; a melancholic air
Half-masks them, while the sun-warmed windows
      stare
Affronted on the purposeless parade
Of pigmy visitors. In postures glum,
Like exiled Counts the statues mope aloof.
No vultured banner flaps above the roof:
And loyal gardens, drowsing in the hum
And slant of lapsing afternoon, seem sad.
  Fountains upheave pale plumes against the
      sky,
Murmuring, " *Their Majesties came sauntering
      by—*

Was it but yesterday? " . . . Proud fountains sigh
Toward the long glades in golden foliage clad,
" *Kürfürsts could do no wrong* " . . . And the woods reply,
" *Take them for what they were, they weren't so bad!* "

STORM ON FIFTH AVENUE

A sallow waiter brings me six huge oysters . . .
Gloom shutters up the sunset with a plague
Of unpropitious twilight jagged asunder
By flashlight demonstrations. *Gee, what a peach
Of a climate!* (Pardon slang : these sultry storms
Afflict me with neurosis : rumbling thunder
Shakes my belief in academic forms.)

An oyster-coloured atmospheric rumpus
Beats up to blot the sunken daylight's gildings.
Against the looming cloud-bank, ivory-pale,
Stand twenty-storied blocks of office buildings.
Snatched upward on a gust, lost news-sheets sail
Forlorn in lone arena of mid-air ;
Flapping like melancholy kites, they scare
My gaze, a note of wildness in the scene.

Out on the pattering side-walk, people hurry
For shelter, while the tempest swoops to scurry
Across to Brooklyn. Bellying figures clutch

At wide-brimmed hats and bend to meet the
    weather,
Alarmed for fresh-worn silks and flurried feather.
Then hissing deluge splashes down to beat
The darkly glistening flatness of the street.
Only the cars nose on through rain-lashed twi-
    light :
Only the Sherman statue, angel-guided,
Maintains its mock-heroic martial gesture.

*   *   *

A sallow waiter brings me beans and pork . . .
Outside there's fury in the firmament.
Ice-cream, of course, will follow; and I'm con-
    tent.
O Babylon ! O Carthage ! O New York !

CONCERT-INTERPRETATION

(LE SACRE DU PRINTEMPS)

The Audience pricks an intellectual Ear . . .
Stravinsky . . . Quite the Concert of the Year!

*　　　*　　　*

Forgetting now that none-so-distant date
When they (or folk facsimilar in state
Of mind) first heard with hisses—hoots—guffaws
This abstract Symphony; (they booed because
Stravinsky jumped their Wagner palisade
With modes that seemed cacophonous and
　　　queer;)
Forgetting now the hullabaloo they made,
The Audience pricks an intellectual Ear.

*　　　*　　　*

Bassoons begin . . . Sonority envelops
Our auditory innocence; and brings
To Me, I must admit, some drift of things
Omnific, seminal, and adolescent.

396

Polyphony through dissonance develops
A serpent-conscious Eden, crude but pleasant;
While vibro-atmospheric copulations
With mezzo-forte mysteries of noise
Prelude Stravinsky's statement of the joys
That unify the monkeydom of nations.

* * *

This matter is most indelicate indeed !
Yet one perceives no symptom of stampede.
The Stalls remain unruffled : craniums gleam
Swept by a storm of pizzicato chords :
Elaborate ladies reassure their lords
With lifting brows that signify " Supreme ! "
While orchestrated gallantry of goats
Impugns the astigmatic programme-note.

In the Grand Circle one observes no sign
Of riot : peace prevails along the line.
And in the Gallery, cargoed to capacity
No tremor bodes eruptions and alarms.
They are listening to this not-quite-new audacity
As though it were by someone dead,—like
 Brahms.

* * *

But savagery pervades Me; I am frantic
With corybantic rupturing of laws.
Come, dance, and seize this clamorous chance to
    function
Creatively,—abandoning compunction
In anti-social rhapsodic applause !
Lynch the conductor ! Jugulate the drums !
Butcher the brass ! Ensanguinate the strings !
Throttle the flutes ! . . . Stravinsky's April comes
With pitiless pomp and pain of sacred springs . . .
Incendiarize the Hall with resinous fires
Of sacrificial fiddles scorched and snapping ! . . .

*　　　　　*　　　　　*

Meanwhile the music blazes and expires ;
And the delighted Audience is clapping.

FALLING ASLEEP

Voices moving about in the quiet house :
Thud of feet and a muffled shutting of doors :
Everyone yawning. Only the clocks are alert.

Out in the night there's autumn-smelling gloom
Crowded with whispering trees; across the park
A hollow cry of hounds like lonely bells :
And I know that the clouds are moving across
    the moon;
The low, red, rising moon. Now herons call
And wrangle by their pool; and hooting owls
Sail from the wood above pale stooks of oats.

Waiting for sleep, I drift from thoughts like
    these;
And where to-day was dream-like, build my
    dreams.
Music . . . there was a bright white room below,
And someone singing a song about a soldier,
One hour, two hours ago : and soon the song

Will be "*last night*": but now the beauty
    swings
Across my brain, ghost of remembered chords
Which still can make such radiance in my dream
That I can watch the marching of my soldiers,
And count their faces; faces; sunlit faces.

Falling asleep . . . the herons, and the hounds . .
September in the darkness; and the world
I've known; all fading past me into peace.

EDWARD SHANKS

TO THE UNIMPLORED BELOVED

Remain, for me, chaste, unapproached, unstirred,
Never from me shall you hear any word,
   Asking that you should give me what I give :
To-day I speak to you, but even to-day
You shall know it is not you to whom I say
   I love you, and shall love you while I live.

Once in these years my lips have touched your
      lips,
O will-benumbing sweetness !—so one sips
   Timidly a magical, an immortal wine
Too strong for human bodies, only to try,
Saying that if I die, one can but die,
   But if I live, that dangerous joy was mine.

Now move no footstep from your place, do not
Repeat that moment nor by any jot
   Of speech or touch of hand or glance of eye
Show to me any more than common kindness,
But go your lovely way in lovely blindness
   —You the still seen, the enraptured seër I.

For gathered flowers grow limp, bright-dusted
     wings
Of handled butterflies grow shabby things,
  The mistress once enjoyed becomes a woman
—Attentive, kindly, comforting, too near,
Till what was magic is no more than dear—
  So, knowing I am, I will not think you human.

Some men love beauties they have found in
    books,
Or who from pictures with unfading looks
  Gaze out upon this changing, fading life,
I you, and thus, and I would have you be
Ever the same and still remote from me,
  Only an image, neither lover nor wife.

THE SHADOW

Death, would I feared not thee,
But ever can I see
Thy mutable shadow thrown
Upon the walls of Life's warm, cheerful room.
Companioned or alone,
I feel the presence of that following gloom,
Like one who vaguely knows
Behind his back the shade his body throws—
'Tis not thy shadow only, 'tis my own!

I face towards the light
That rises fair and bright
Over wide fields asleep,
But still I know that stealthy darkness there
Close at my heels doth creep,
My ghostly company, my haunting care;
And if the light be strong
Before my eyes, through pleasant hours and long,
Then, then, the shadow is most black and deep.

THE SHADOWGRAPH

I play a game that children play,
  Tracing your shadow on the wall;
But on the wall the shadows stray
  As the wood-flames flare and fall.

Your image rests in quiet now,
  A moment. Quickly I can draw
The profile, chin, mouth, nose and brow
  And close-coiled hair. But what I saw,

Ere half the line is traced, has gone :
  The pencil must begin anew,
And all so painfully begun
  But wastes the wall with scrawls untrue.

Until at last the lamp is brought,
  The game is done, and I can see
The tangled scribble I have wrought
  Grimacing at me mockingly.

MEMORY

In silence and in darkness memory wakes
Her million sheathèd buds and breaks
That day-long winter when the light and noise
And hard bleak breath of the outward looking
    will
Made barren her tender soil, when every voice
Of her million airy birds was muffled or still.

One bud-sheath breaks :
One sudden voice awakes.
What change grew in our hearts seeing one night
That moth-winged ship drifting across the bay,
  Her broad sail dimly white
On cloudy waters and hills as vague as they?
Some new thing touched our spirits with distant
    delight,
Half seen, half noticed, as we loitered down,
Talking in whispers, to the little town,
  Down from the narrow hill
—Talking in whispers, for the air so still
Imposed its stillness on our lips and made

407

A quiet equal with the equal shade
That filled the slanting walk. That phantom now
Slides with slack canvas and unwhispering prow
Through the dark sea that this dark room has
     made.

Or the night of the closed eyes will turn to day
And all day's colours start out of the grey.
The sun burns on the water. The tall hills
Push up their shady groves into the sky
And fail and cease where the intense light spills
Its parching torrent on the gaunt and dry
Rock of the farther mountains, whence the snow
That softened their harsh edges long is gone
   And nothing tempers now
The hot flood falling on the barren stone.

   O memory, take and keep
All that my eyes, your servants, bring you
     home—
Those other days beneath the low white dome
   Of smooth-spread clouds that creep
   As slow and soft as sleep,
When shade grows pale and the cypress stands
     upright,
   Distinct in the cool light,
Rigid and solid as a dark, hewn stone;

And many another night
That melts in darkness on the narrow quays
And changes every colour and every tone
And soothes the water to a softer ease,
When under constellations coldly bright
The homeward sailors sing their way to bed
On ships that motionless in harbour float.
The circling harbour-lights flash green and red;
And, out beyond, a steady travelling boat
Breaking the swell with slow industrious oars
    At each stroke pours
Pale lighted water from the lifted blade.
Now in the painted houses all around
    Slow darkening windows call
The empty unwatched middle of the night.
The tide's few inches rise without a sound.
On the black promontory's windless head,
The last awake, the fireflies rise and fall
And tangle up their dithering skeins of light.

O memory, take and keep
All that my eyes, your servants, bring you home !
    Thick through the changing year
The unexpected, rich-charged moments come.
    That you 'twixt wake and sleep
In the lids of the closed eyes shall make appear.

This is life's certain good,
Though in the end it be not good at all
    When the dark end arises
And the stripped, startled spirit must let fall
    The amulets that could
Prevail with life's but not death's sad devices.

Then, like a child from whom an older child
    Forces its gathered treasures,
Its beads and shells and strings of withered
        flowers,
    Tokens of recent pleasures,
The soul must lose in eyes weeping and wild
    Those prints of vanished hours.

TO THE UNKNOWN VOICE

Speak once again, forgotten voice!
How, how gladly would I hear thee
Guide my blind and mortal choice,
Yet long months I come not near thee.
Whither hast thou then removed,
Or did I never hear thee?
Was that whispering in the mind
Which with sense intent I divined
Only the stir of blood in pulses aching?
Hast thou never to my ear
Stooped thy sweet mouth, my spirit waking?
Speak now, if speak thou canst. The hot blood
   shaking
Temples and arteries I know,
And in the loud confusion I shall know thee.
Speak and I will hear,
Heart, will and spirit all shall show thee.

Ah, no, no, no!
In the vast echoing cave

Floored by green earth and roofed by empty sky
Nothing but wind and wave
And no reply
Save vain reverberation of my cry.

Forgotten voice, speak, speak again,
Clearer than winds or waves or men.
Like a lost friend in countries far away,
Thou hast been for so long a day :
Yet rise again, yet speak again to me ;
I dwindle, wanting thee !

THE HAUNTING

The owl that lives in the hole in the oak
 Need fear no more your prying hand
That once on his daylight slumber broke
 In a game he never could understand.

You and I will go together no more
 And, setting our hands on the clock's loud
  chime,
Strike four o'clock at twenty to four
 That the village may live by a fancied time.

The apples will hang on the drooping bough
 And you will not pluck at them as you pass :
You never go down the pathway now
 Leading your pony out to grass.

You are gone from there and I could not stay
 In a place where ever I seemed to see
A ghost that slipped through the winter day
 Too quickly to stop and speak to me.

For the ghosts of the living walk, I know,
  More often than those of the peaceful dead :
Have I not through those alleys seen you go,
  A tall, slim girl, with a proud, small head?

If I walk, a ghost, in the garden yet,
  In the ghost of *our* garden let it be :
With last year's rain may the lawns be wet,
  And spirits of leaves on a phantom tree.

Let the sap of the wounded sumach bleed
  Where we broke the boughs last year to pass,
Let the poppy rattle her dried-up seed
  And last year's fir-cones lie on the grass.

This year I know not, I will not know,
  If new flowers bloom for the voyaging bee,
If here the bushes more thickly grow
  Or there a sapling is sprung to a tree.

There must be no change. If I found a change,
  Then the phantom-I might find you there,
Not a ghost but the new year's you, and strange,
  And the last year's you not anywhere.

THE FAIRY'S CHILD

I have known love, and thrice or more
  Has beauty on my pleading smiled :
For one or two my heart was sore
  And one I loved was a fairy's child.

Fairies are neither good nor evil
  But strange : they follow different laws.
Fool that I was in her to level
  Human effect and fairy cause !

With that deception sick and spent
  I wept alone, but now I see
She was, though wide her footsteps went,
  Faithful to love if not to me.

SONNET

He who so long a shadow contemplated
  (The storm being done, a long stilled voice
      hath said)
Finds himself in the end with a shadow mated
  And, quick though it move, a shadow is but
      dead.
We love not women but the images
  Ourselves have made of Beauty, Kindness,
      Youth:
Vain shapes that any candle throws may please
  Till unexpected movement tells the truth.
It was not you I loved, it was not you!
  It was your beauty was the flickering fire
That on the wall I watched so eagerly threw
  A gibing shadow of my own desire.
But, should I now to the real woman turn,
Might true love from that first true sight be born?

THE BITTEN GRASS

How coldly I survey
This windless corner in the bleached and wintry
    gorse
Which was our shelter once, day after day.
But now my horse
Is halted here by habit, not the rein,
And here we stay,
I dreaming coldly back, he reaching for the grass,
In him no hunger and in me no pain,
But in us both desires that idly pass.
How sluggish is the beast, he will not move,
How sluggish is my heart that has outgrown its
    love !

So short a time, four seasons have not gone—
This, if my heart forgets, my eyes must know.
Grass does not grow
In autumn or in winter : till the sun
Comes overhead again, there still shall be

These white, dry, bitten stalks to testify
That here long summer mornings we would lie
While the ponies grazed beside us peaceably.
These bitten stalks, a circle eaten dry
And trampled down, this was our shelter, this
Was where you drew me down, begging another
    kiss.

THE LUCKY DAY

(Gliding Competition on Itford Hill,
October 21st, 1922.)

Come down, belovèd, from the crowded hill :
The darkening air grows chill,
Though still the man-bird sways from spur to
    spur,
Triumphant in the dusk, and still below
The motor-horns applaud with harsh hurray.
We have seen Fokker going to and fro
His patient hundred yards of conquered air
And still at every turning halt and sway :
We have seen Raynham slide
A mile before the wind and slip and fall :
We have seen spurred by all
The wind's invisible and nervous side.
And now away,
The last jog homeward ends our holiday.
Kick Polly's ribs and come. The hillside way
Gives us a slow and careful journey down.
Come, now you see,
Far off, the crowned lights of the distant town

Beckon us home to stable and to tea.
Love loves the lucky, so they say,
And I have had my luck to-day,
Seeing you when I thought we had said good-
    bye.
To-morrow I am going away,
But this last luck new knots will tie
In the handkerchief of your memory.

I do not trust you yet
Not to forget;
But better I should go and take my chance.
It is thought that absence sometimes may en-
    hance
The lover's gifts for whomso he may love
And that his image more may move
Her mind than presence or than bold advance
Of speech or touch. So think I not, but now
To-morrow with an easier heart I go,
Luck having blessed me,
Though on this hill's open and crowded brow
Only luck has kissed me.

We have seen Raynham slide
A mile before the wind and slip and fall,
And also, side by side,
Maneyrolle and Gray

Against a darkening and a stormier day
Ride out the sudden squall.
These men, in love with air—though who knows
    why ?—
Trust luck to see them through the enterprise
And in the risk discover ecstasy,
Being better lucky than wise.
As they on unknown currents fall or rise,
So I on luck or on your favour,
Both as unknown to science, as uncharted,
As the wild air's behaviour,
Will stake, glad-hearted,
All that I am or may be, all that is I.

Love loves the lucky, so they say,
And luck has been my friend to-day. . . .

WOMAN'S SONG

No more upon my bosom rest thee,
Too often have my hands caressed thee,
  My lips thou knowest well, too well;
Lean to my heart no more thine ear
My spirit's living truth to hear
  —It has no more to tell.

In what dark night, in what strange night,
Burnt to the butt the candle's light
  That lit our room so long?
I do not know, I thought I knew
How love could be both sweet and true:
  I also thought it strong.

Where has the flame departed?   Where,
Amid the empty waste of air,
  Is that which dwelt with us?
Was it a fancy?   Did we make
Only a show for dead love's sake,
  It being so piteous?

No more against my bosom press thee,
Seek no more that my hands caress thee,
  Leave the sad lips thou hast known so well;
If to my heart thou lean thine ear
There grieving thou shalt only hear
  Vain murmuring of an empty shell.

W. J. TURNER

THE SEARCH FOR THE NIGHTINGALE

Beside a stony, shallow stream I sat
In a deep gully underneath a hill.
I watched the water trickle down dark moss
And shake the tiny boughs of maidenhair,
And billow on the bodies of cold stone.
And sculptured clear
Upon the shoulder of that aerial peak
Stood trees, the fragile skeletons of light,
High in a bubble blown
Of visionary stone.

Under that azurine transparent arch
The hill, the rocks, the trees
Were still and dreamless as the printed wood
Black on the snowy page.
It was the song of some diviner bird
Than this still country knew :
The words were twigs of burnt and blackened
    trees
From which there trilled a voice,
Shadowy and faint, as though it were the song
The water carolled as it flowed along.

Lifting my head, I gazed upon the world,
Carved in the breathless heat as in a gem,
And watched the parroquets green-feathered fly
Through crystal vacancy, and perch in trees
That glittered in a thin, blue, haze-like dream,
And the voice faded, though the water dinned
Against the stones its dimming memory.
And I ached then
To hear that song burst out upon that scene,
Startling an earth where it had never been.

And then I came unto an older world.
The woods were damp, the sun
Shone in a watery mist, and soon was gone;
The trees were thick with leaves, heavy and old,
The sky was grey, and blue, and like the sea
Rolling with mists and shadowy veils of foam.
I heard the roaring of an ancient wind
Among the elms and in the tattered pines;
Lighting pale hollows in the cloud-dark sky,
A ghostly ship, the Moon, flew scudding by.

" O is it here," I cried, " that bird that sings
So that the traveller in his frenzy weeps? "
It was the autumn of the year, and leaves
Fell with a dizzy moan, and all the trees

Roared like the sea at my small impotent voice.
And if the bird was there it did not sing,
And I knew not its haunts, or where it went,
But carven stood and raved !
In that old wood that dripped upon my face
Upturned below, pale in its passionate chase.

And years went by, and I grew slowly cold :
I had forgotten what I once had sought,
There are no passions that do not grow dim,
And like a fire imagination sinks
Into the ashes of the mind's cold grate.
And if I dreamed, I dreamed of that far land,
That coast of pearl upon a summer sea,
Whose frail trees in unruffled amber sleep,
Gaudy with jewelled birds, whose feathers spray
Bright founts of colour through the tranquil day.

The hill, the gully, and the stony stream
I had not thought on when this spring I sat
In a strange room with candles guttering down
Into the flickering silence. From the Moon
Among the trees still-wreathed upon the sky
There came the sudden twittering of a ghost.
And I stept out from darkness, and I saw
The great pale sky immense, transparent, filled

With boughs and mountains and wide-shining
   lakes
Where stillness, crying in a thin voice, breaks.

It was the voice of that imagined bird.
I saw the gully and that ancient hill,
The water trickling down from Paradise
Shaking the tiny boughs of maidenhair.
There sat the dreaming boy.
And O! I wept to see that scene again,
To read the black print on that snowy page,
I wept and all was still.
No shadow came into that sun-steeped glen,
No sound of earth, no voice of living men.

Was it a dream or was it that in me
A God awoke and gazing on his dream
Saw that dream rise and gaze into its soul,
Finding, Narcissus-like, its image there :
A Song, a transitory Shape on water blown,
Descending down the bright cascades of time,
The shadowiest-flowering, ripple-woven bloom
As ghostly as still waters' unseen foam
That lies upon the air, as that song lay
Within my heart on one far summer day?

Carved in the azure air white peacocks fly,
Their fanning wings stir not the crystal trees,
Bright parrots fade through dimming turquoise
    days,
And music scrolls its lightning calm and bright
On the pale sky where thunder cannot come.
Into that world no ship has ever sailed,
No seaman gazing with hand-shaded eyes
Has ever seen its shore whiten the waves.
But to that land the Nightingale has flown,
Leaving bright treasure on this calm air blown.

TENT, MY DEAREST TENT

My soul is like a wandering Arab
  Who, solitary, brings
His house among the desert stars
  On hill or plain, by palm or brook,
And 'mid the loneliness of ways
  Thus to his comfort sings :

Among the Universe's winds
  Tent, my dearest tent,
Thou dost house a quiet breath,
A soft breath, a little breath,
  A leaf upon the tree
  Making a quiet lament.

Leaf, thou art a rib of Wind
  That trembles through the sky,
Quivering into a grosser dress,
  A dress of flesh, a body—
O universal Gale of life,
  Thy fluttering leaf am I.

And—light of Moon and Sun—
  Thou, Foliage, and Snows
(Fading upon this star where I
  Were else dark, pitched in dark),
Bright Fabric of my walls,
  That in the darkness blows,

Amidst the wilderness of Space
  Thy glimmer may be spent,
But there are other lights that burn
  'Mid other hills and other snows;
And somewhere once more shall be pitched
  Tent, my dearest tent!

My soul is like a wandering Arab
  Who crossing hill and plain
Under night's glittering suns shall pitch
  His tent of life, his fluttering sign,
And when Dawn rises on the world
  It shall have gone again.

SORROWING FOR CHILDHOOD
DEPARTED

Who is there among us who has found the key
   Of the treasure that is locked in the hearts of
      men?
Only the poet lonely in his chamber
   Or the man remembering his childhood again.

Hearing gay voices, my heart is hollow,
   An empty room with bright colours on the
      walls;
The speech of my brother is no more than a
      traffic
   That remote and coldly on my dull brain falls.

I am deaf to the song in the speech of my fellows,
   I have outwitted my childhood's desires;
And where have I travelled that to the far horizon
   Dead in the landscape are earth's bright fires?

Didst thou ever murder, Macbeth, thy sorrow,
   Didst thou ever murder thy soul's young joy,

Thou hadst never flinched from the life of
    another,
  Thou hadst but with laughter stol'n from him
    a toy!

Would that a Spirit had stolen from me
  The glittering baubles of my cunning mind,
And left me the sweet forest of my wondering
    childhood,
  Its transparent water in tall trees enshrined.

Then was I happy. Love was my companion;
  I was in communion with star and stream;
With bird and with flower I was linked in rapture,
  We stared at each other—the valley's dream.

Out of the mountains we were carven,
  Birds and flowers, stream, rock and child—
O but I belong there! I am torn from my body,
  In that far-away forest it lies exiled!

  There falls the water transparently shining,
  Hangs there a flower that blooms in my eyes.
Long have I been ready! let me go thither,
  And unloosen my limbs to those dream-
    coloured skies.

O that it were possible! but that land has
  vanished;
 The magic of that valley has crumbled away;
Bright crowds are there only, the mind's cold
  idola;
 And my footprints on the dead ground startle
  the day.

DOROTHY WELLESLEY

WINTER FLAME

Sun-blistered ships on opal seas,
Pacific stars spilt round the skies,
What have I now to do with these
Who know the wonder of your eyes?

I rose and went in search of pain,
When the gay spring passed through the land;
Oh, clamorous spring, that cried in vain
The pulse and magic of your hand.

Then, sudden sleet and blossom flew
On currents of the glittering gale,
And the starch-hyacinth's spikes of blue
Flared proudly through the fallen hail.

But island spring and starry wake
Left love asleep, made calm a crime,
Oh, fretting heart that longed to break,
That broke and bloomed in dark and rime.

Now, slow teams climb the winter flank
New-ribboned of the upland track;
Criss-cross the heavens blanched and blank
Work down the wind with flying wrack

From fieldside wood, and forward blown
Go branch and leaf and flying mane,
While horses move deliberate down
To strawstacks by the sunken lane.

Or by a smooth and rook-specked hill
The sculptured marble clouds are curled,
Like Genii of unholy will
Rising in smoke above the world.

Now, light and shade, from cloud or rift,
May rollick forth with banners brave,
And from a field the wind may lift
And chase the colour that it gave

So gallantly two breaths ago.
Or sheep-cries rack a blinded scene,
When sheets of fog are twisted low,
And strangled earth is robbed of green.

Now, on the hedge the Traveller's Joy
Clambers like pipe smoke up the air,
And skeined along the liquid sky
Each evening tree is like a prayer.

Now, in the fast oncoming night,
Beneath the steely flying snows,
The garden stretches black and white,
That gave the lupin and the rose.

What care if tropic harbours swirl,
Grape-coloured in the morning shine,
Or through the red pomegranates curl
The swags and tangles of the vine?

What care that beauty dwells supreme
In men and women, towns and ships,
Set dark against the gold of dream :
Temples, bright boats, and carven lips?

What care for hillsides where the heat
Puffs acrid from the glowing stone?
I've heard beneath my head the beat
Of your strong heart, which is my own.

What care though fire and colour flared
Eternal from the coral skies,
To one who in this darkness dared
To claim the secrets of your eyes?

LOST LANE

Catkins, like caterpillars slung a-row,
Roof over, with sloe blossom, this lost track
And speckle it with shadow. Deep in June
Afloat with weed and wrack,
It sways, a sunken garden in a tide
Of apple green, and there
Each evening, at the light end of the lane
Cassiopeia, Lady in her Chair,
Sits light and elegant, watching with me
The Zodiac blaze on the twelve compass points :
The spiteful Scorpion; sentimental Twins;
The Crab with crazy joints;
The Water Carrier, watering the dark
With drench of diamonds; jewelled Archer, wild
With hair of scattered gold; Goat, Virgin, Scales
Aswarm on space like spattered bees; once styled
From dark Chaldean towers the gates of suns,
Triumphal arches.

                Here, where labourers pass,
Striding the stile, the polished bar has caught
Those royal highways in a looking-glass,

Holding them prisoner till the autumn comes.
Then with a swoop and glitter,
Then with a gale the Sickle gets aswing
Across the sky, to reap the stars, to litter
With spirtled stars the fallow and the corn,
The villages we know; till roof and spire,
And elm trees, massed like ostrich feather plumes,
Are streaked and shot with fire.

They fall beyond the fields.

                              Arise, pursue
Sea-ward, and sift the backwash of a tide
For starfish from the sky,
Among wet light of shells, rose, russet, pied.

They fall beyond the sea.
On thundering sea holms, through white ribs of
    hulls
Skied up on ridges (Ships that followed them),
Watched by dark eyes of skulls.

HORSES ON THE FELL

That too is England; there the fell
Encloses tarns in craters, there
The walls of slate form pits of hell,
Black pools shut inward from the air.

The ponies know the paths, their neat,
Their tiny hooves, on sheer descents,
Tread circumspectly, and the peat
Rings hollow on the thudding pents.

The burns blow chains of bubbles, spray
The moss, pin-cushioned all around,
Swung bells and stars are drenched all day,
Rock gardens hang above the sound.

For water goes with twists and turns
Abruptly down the dale,
Till all the shrill and flurrying burns
Swirl down, majestic, to the Swale.

There quartz and boulder, slung askew,
Topple and slither from the screes,
While stone escarpments ribbed with yew
Form tiers of twilight palaces.

But far above, the scud and hail
Patters and raps on humps of stones,
White objects strewn among the shale,
Sheep skulls with teeth, and stranger bones.

. . . .

The horses stand on stormy skies
Hind quarters windward, like a thong
Their manes are lashed across their eyes;
On the streaked sunsets go headlong
The sounding splendour of their trails,
Before the dawns, light windy teams,
Winged stallions of the Nordic tales,
They are not horses, they are dreams.

For see! Beneath storm buffeted stars
Their flanks are phosphorescent, then
What Holy Twins, what Songs, what Wars
Possess them, through the sleep of men?

See! Taut with slashing tails unshorn
They wait in twilight, dappled, dun,
Till in the great white spate of dawn
They are the Horses of the Sun.

They drink the fountains, leap on death,
Chimera, Hero-friends they know,—
Fiery and sacred is their breath,
And like the whirlwind they must go
While lasts the world, upon the heights.
Their hooves ring heavenward silver shod,
They strike the lightning, scattering lights,
This is the cavalcade of God.

OLD CALL

Give back the adolescent world, the prime
Fierce currents of the blood; the rough, the harsh,
The crag, the waste, the marsh.
In these low-lighted flowery rooms they call,
Those wild gold eyes that gleam in woods of time,
By wide warm rivers darkened by giant leaves,
Unconquered, from a rank-breathed animal,
Beholding faiths and valours that we knew
With hot dawn-drips, unsentimental eyes.

Here, Hamlet-like, we whisper: " What is
    true ? "
Cry fearsome : " Where is God ? " and inly know
We have nor war, nor peace, nor friend, nor foe.
Lives that crouch back, to charge your agony,
Loves that draw back, to drive on your desire,
Know blood and sweat, give me the forest cry,
The circled stones about the friendly fire,
The torrent, and the faring, and the laughter,
    The sleep that follows after.

I'll seek the spaces void of all but wings,
That beat up wind, or plane before a gale;
Or take the mountain trail
Across the granite Himalayan gate,
Where, peaks above the gentians and the lings,
Undreamed of seeds fly feckless, and the slight
Celestial Poppies rise from shale and slate.
Or ride a horse towards a gaping morn,
Watching his patient ears against the light.

Or board a grain-ship chartered for the Horn,
Where green seas rear to ceilings overhead,
To laugh at and to challenge, so that dread
Of pain itself is purged, washed off the soul,
Vanquished forever; so the waves which flack
The foam against the flesh shall make us whole
From fear of death forever; on such a deck
Win back the battle-faith for life; and after
    Greet the great sleep with laughter.

IOLO ANEURIN WILLIAMS

AT A MUSIC HALL

" When dreams come true," the ballad singer
    sang,
And loudly through the hall the plaudits rang;
For some folk's time has been so ill-employed
They've hardly glanced at either Jung or Freud.

A DULL DAY

How break this cloud that hangs to-day
 About my stifled mind?
How wake to life these muffled ears,
 These eyes so nearly blind?

The world, I know, lies beautiful
 To-day, as every day :—
I see the sparrows from the tree
 Shaking a raindrop spray;

And times there are when sight of this
 My inmost soul would wring
With joy for the fresh changefulness
 Of each familiar thing.

But not to-day, when all my soul
 Knows nought but dull and grey—
Yet yearns for a vague loveliness
 Ten million worlds away.

QUESTION AND ANSWER

Lady, lady now you lie
Under a black and earthy sky,
To lighten which no light clouds pass—
There on the dark side of the grass;
Do you not miss our fair and wide
Life with its many-lighted pride,
Wherewith your coloured beauty vied?

Friend, though fair my sight, maybe,
Sight was never joy to me,
And dark is a shawl that's kindly laid
On eyes Life could but make afraid.

THE BLACK LAKE

As one the eye mirrors not
    But the heart remembers,
In the dark lake's deepest grot
    Live the sun's embers.

Black 'mid the mountains steep
    In the cleft where they caught her,
Prisoned and still and deep
    Lies the lake water.

The sun o'er the hill's high edge
    Scarce looks in a summer;
Safe holds the lake the pledge
    Of that dear rare-comer.

Safe 'neath her mantle black
    The light lies treasured,
Till again that lovely track
    By her lover is measured.

SPRING SUNSHINE

To fiery sun, blue firmament,
  To golden bloom, and emerald frond,
Oh ! what a piteous instrument
  Am I, who only half respond !

TO " ANON "

May Clio never come to rout you
  From that kind shade around you hung :
Enough, to know one thing about you—
  The cadenced beauty of your tongue.

A PRAYER

Non omnis moriar. I pray
   That, when I'm dead a hundred years,
Whate'er of me yet lives may say,
   " Joy won his laughter, Grief his tears."

FRANCIS BRETT YOUNG

SEASCAPE

Over that morn hung heaviness, until,
Near sunless noon, we heard the ship's bell
    beating
A melancholy staccato on dead metal;
Saw the bare-footed watch come running aft;
Felt, far below, the sudden telegraph jangle
Its harsh metallic challenge, thrice repeated:
Stand by. Half-speed ahead. Slow. Stop her!
    They stopped.
The plunging pistons sank like a stopt heart:
She held, she swayed, a hulk, a hollow carcass
Of blistered iron that the grey-green, waveless,
Unruffled tropic waters slapped languidly.
Burial at sea! A Portuguese official . . .
Poor fever-broken devil from Mozambique:
Came on half-tight: the doctor calls it heat-
    stroke.
Why do they travel steerage? It's the exchange:
So many million reis to the pound!
What did he look like? No one ever saw him:
Took to his bunk, and drank and drank and died.

They're ready! Silence!

               We clustered to the rail,
Curious and half-ashamed. The well-deck spread
A comfortable gulf of segregation
Between ourselves and death. *Burial at sea* . . .
The master holds a black book at arm's length;
His droning voice comes for'ard : *This our
    brother* . . .
We therefore commit his body to the deep
To be turned into corruption . . .

               The bo's'n whispers
Hoarsely behind his hand : *Now, all together!*
The hatch-cover is tilted; a mummy of sail-cloth
Well ballasted with iron shoots clear of the poop;
Falls, like a diving gannet. The green sea closes
Its burnished skin; the snaky swell smoothes
    over . . .
While he, the man of the steerage, goes down,
    down,
Feet-foremost, sliding swiftly down the dim
    water :
Swift to escape
Those plunging shapes with pale, empurpled
    bellies
That swirl and veer about him. He goes down
Unerringly, as though he knew the way

Through green, through gloom, to absolute
    watery darkness,
Where no weed sways nor curious fin quivers :
To the sad, sunless deeps, where, endlessly,
A downward drift of death spreads its wan mantle
In the wave-moulded valleys that shall enfold
    him
Till the sea give up its dead.
There shall he lie dispersed amid great riches :
Such gold, such arrogance, so many bold hearts !
All the sunken armadas pressed to powder
By weight of incredible seas ! That mingled
    wrack
No livening sun shall visit till the crust
Of earth be riven, or this rolling planet
Reel on its axis ; till the moon-chained tides,
Unloosed, deliver up that white Atlantis,
Whose naked peaks shall bleach above the
    slaked
Thirst of Sahara, fringed by weedy tangles
Of Atlas's drown'd cedars, frowning Eastward
To where the sands of India lie cold,
And heaped Himalaya's a rib of coral
Slowly uplifted, grain on grain . . .
                    We dream
Too long ! Another jangle of alarum

Stabs at the engines : *Slow. Half-speed. Full-*
    speed!
The great bearings rumble; the screw churns, frothing
    frothing
Opaque water to downward swelling plumes
Milky as woodsmoke. A shoal of flying-fish
Spurts out like animate spray. The warm breeze
    wakens,
And we pass on, forgetting,
Toward the solemn horizon of bronzed cumulus
That bounds our brooding sea, gathering gloom
That, when night falls, will dissipate in flaws
Of watery lightning, washing the hot sky,
Cleansing all hearts of heat and restlessness,
Until, with day, another blue be born.

THE QUAILS

(In the South of Italy the peasants put out the
eyes of a captured quail so that its cries may
attract the flocks of spring migrants into their
nets.)

All through the night
I have heard the stuttering call of a blind quail,
A caged decoy, under a cairn of stones,
Crying for light as the quails cry for love.

Other wanderers,
Northward from Africa winging on numb pinions,
      dazed
With beating winds and the sobbing of the sea,
Hear, in a breath of sweet land-herbage, the call
Of the blind one, their sister . . .
Hearing their fluttered hearts
Take courage, and they wheel in their dark flight,
Knowing that their toil is over, dreaming to see
The white stubble of Abruzzi smitten with dawn

And spilt grain lying in the furrows, the
    squandered gold
That is the delight of quails in their spring
    mating.

Land scents grow keener,
Penetrating the dank and bitter odour of brine
That whitens their feathers;
Far below, the voice of their sister calls them
To plenty, and sweet water, and fulfilment.
Over the pallid margin of dim seas breaking,
Over the thickening in the darkness that is land,
They fly. Their flight is ended. Wings beat no
    more.
Downward they drift, one by one, like dark
    petals,
Slowly, listlessly falling,
Into the mouth of horror :
The nets. . . .

Where men come trampling and crying with
    bright lanterns,
Plucking their weak, entangled claws from the
    meshes of net,
Clutching the soft brown bodies mottled with
    olive,

Crushing the warm, fluttering flesh, in hands
    stained with blood,
Till their quivering hearts are stilled, and the
    bright eyes,
That are like a polished agate, glaze in death.

But the blind one, in her wicker cage, without
    ceasing
Haunts this night of spring with her stuttering
    call,
Knowing nothing of the terror that walks in
    darkness,
Knowing only that some cruelty has stolen the
    light
That is life, and that she must cry until she dies.

I, in the darkness,
Heard, and my heart grew sick. But I know that
    to-morrow
A smiling peasant will come with a basket of
    quails
Wrapped in vine-leaves, prodding them with
    blood-stained fingers,
Saying, " Signore, you must cook them thus, and
    thus,
Q

With a sprig of basil inside them." And I shall
    thank him,
Carrying the piteous carcases into the kitchen
Without a pang, without shame.

" Why should I be ashamed? Why should I rail
Against the cruelty of men? Why should I pity,
Seeing that there is no cruelty which men can
    imagine
To match the subtle dooms that are wrought
    against them
By blind spores of pestilence : seeing that each
    of us,
Lured by dim hopes, flutters in the toils of death
On a cold star that is spinning blindly through
    space
Into the nets of time? "

So cried I, bitterly thrusting pity aside,
Closing my lids to sleep. But sleep came not,
And pity, with sad eyes,
Crept to my side, and told me
That the life of all creatures is brave and pitiful
Whether they be men, with dark thoughts to vex
    them,
Or birds, wheeling in the swift joys of flight,

Or brittle ephemerids, spinning to death in the
    haze
Of gold that quivers on dim evening waters;
Nor would she be denied.
The harshness died
Within me, and my heart
Was caught and fluttered like the palpitant heart
Of a brown quail, flying
To the call of her blind sister,
And death, in the spring night.

INDEX

INDEX

471

INDEX